CHAPTERS IN
Autism
STORIES OF
Grace

CHAPTERS IN *Autism*
STORIES OF *Grace*

A Devotional for Those
Who Find Themselves
in the Unexpected

LYNN ROSE DUNHAM

CHAPTERS IN AUTISM, STORIES OF GRACE
Copyright © 2025 by Lynn Rose Dunham

Scripture quotations taken from the Holy Bible, King James Version, which is in the public domain.

ISBN: 978-1-4866-2702-8
eBook ISBN: 978-1-4866-2703-5

Word Alive Press
119 De Baets Street Winnipeg, MB R2J 3R9
www.wordalivepress.ca

WORD ALIVE
—P R E S S—

Cataloguing in Publication information can be obtained from Library and Archives Canada.

DEDICATION

This book is lovingly dedicated to my precious family.

To my husband, John. Thank you for being my number one cheerleader! Your loving support has meant the world to me. One of the dearest characteristics I appreciate about you is your impromptu prayer meetings. Whether we're driving down the road or I'm just fretting about a matter, you bring it immediately to the Lord in prayer. The way you stop mid-conversation and pray is something I will never take for granted. I am blessed to have you as my husband.

To my daughter, Katie. Your meek and gentle spirit challenges me to be a better person. Even when my requests for tech support and editing were endless, you never once complained. This project would have been impossible without your patient help. Your ability to put others first is a gift not many people possess. God has great plans ahead for your life. I am blessed to have you as my daughter.

To my son, Benjamin. Although you don't realize it, you are the one who has taught me to trust God in the unexpected. The road at times has been tiring, for both of us, but with each tiny accomplishment our celebrations have been all the sweeter. One day in heaven we will have that conversation I can only long for on this earth. I am blessed to have you as my son.

And to the head of my family, Jesus Christ. Your faithfulness is completely undeserved. Your grace for every chapter of my life is a priceless gift. I am beyond blessed to call You my Lord.

Contents

This is the Lord's doing; it is marvellous in
our eyes. This is the day which the Lord
hath made; we will rejoice and be glad in it.
(Psalms 118:23–24)

PREFACE

Growing up as the Avon lady's daughter, lip gloss and "flipped back" hair were my two main staples in life. Shallow as it may sound, I was positive that, with a curling iron in one hand and a hair dryer in the other, nothing could get between me and my dreams.

Yet let's face it: even with "fuzzy filters" and herbal-scented shampoo, life still gets messy.

As narratives unfold, we learn, we grow… and we learn some more. Reflecting on my own faith walk, nothing prepared me to have a profoundly learning-disabled and severely autistic son. More than thirty years after this journey began, I trust that I have grown to be a more compassionate human being.

Unlike in my teen years, my latest makeup tip goes like this: "Tears and mascara are a really bad idea." Through the good, the bad, and the unexpected, I invite you to join me in exploring these chapters of autism and stories of grace.

FOREWORD

Early on an ordinary Sunday morning, I walked into our worship centre and I saw her sitting alone in her regular spot, soaking in those precious moments that happen during the pre-service worship band practice.

Hesitant to interrupt her private worship, yet desirous to take advantage of this rare space in time to get to know her, I walked across the room and sat on the chair beside her.

It wasn't as if I didn't know Lynn. Up to that point, we had shared masked (anyone else remember those pandemic days?) casual conversations in the foyer of our church and I'd admire how lovely and put together she was. I also had an inkling that there was something worth taking the time to explore beneath that lovely surface, that there was a story to be told.

And there was.

The story was of her son, Ben, and a family linking arms, hearts, and faith through the many unknown chapters of autism.

Lynn has skillfully captured grace-filled snapshots of her story in the pages of this book. With great vulnerability, she shares the struggles, pain, disappointment, and daily grind of a life she didn't picture for herself when she became a mom.

But praise God, her story is bigger than that. Better said, her God is bigger than that.

Lynn's story is her testimony of the Lord's grace, mercy, provision, presence, protection, strength, and source of joy in every single tiny detail.

Her circumstances may be different from yours and mine, but none of us are strangers to struggles, pain, disappointment, or wrestling with the daily assignments God has given us.

As you read this book, I pray that you will be encouraged and reminded that God is much bigger than the circumstances of your story. I pray that the Scripture you encounter and the practical wisdom Lynn shares will infuse you with greater faith, courage, and strength to take the next trust-filled step in your own journey.

Lynn, I once told you that you had a book in you. You did.

May the chapters of autism and stories of grace you have penned be used of God beyond anything you could imagine—for His glory alone.

You are loved!

Your friend and pastor's wife,
Kathy Butryn
Director of Discipleship and Administration
The Bridge Whitby Church

WHO REMEMBERS THE CAT ON THE POSTER?

In 1998, Canada lost some of its glow. A beloved department store, Kmart, packed up its wares and headed back to the United States. How could they possibly do this to us? We considered this store a part of our lives, our DNA, our family… well maybe not *family*—but just the same, we were left high and dry.

More than twenty-five years have passed since that mass exodus, yet I can still say, "I miss Kmart." From the scuffed linoleum floors to the cubed jello in the cafeteria, it all tells a story. I even miss the smell of Kmart, that undeniable mixture of plastic, perfume, and French fries. Call me a sentimental fool, but I long for the simplicity of those days, a kinder, sweeter, more gentle way of life. Okay, *gentle* may not be the operative word, especially when I toss out this next little flashback. Prepare yourself, and take a deep breath…

Anyone else remember "the blue-light special"? Ah, to once again hear the crackle of the store intercom, followed by the nasally voice of a department manager and the ring of those practically Shakespearean words: "Blue-light special in aisle seven!" Immediately every red-blooded woman, the tall and the small, would white-knuckle their shopping carts, grab junior's hand, and race towards what was bound to be the bargain of the century.

Goosebumps, right?

Strangely enough, it wasn't about what we bought. For that matter, it didn't have anything to do with whether we even needed the item. It was more about the moment, the frenzy, the story, the laugh we would share… all under a simple blue light hanging on a trolley cart.

If you've stuck with me this far, I hope the nostalgia bug has perhaps bitten you too. Or maybe you're rolling your eyes. Either way, I thank you for sticking with me and humbly request that you indulge me in just one more Kmart story.

When I was a kid, I would head over to the toy department and thumb my way through the large collection of posters. Peace signs, blacklight motifs, heartthrobs, and brightly coloured artwork were all there for the taking. Catchphrases like "Keep on trucking" and "Give peace a chance" dazzled the eyes. What can I say? It was the seventies and we were feeling groovy.

Being a good church girl, I paid no heed to rock group posters. Okay, I must confess to perhaps taking the odd glance at Donny Osmond, but only for a moment… maybe two. But the poster I simply adored was that of a bewildered cat desperately clinging to a bending branch with the words "Hang in there, baby!" printed boldly at the bottom. Wow! To my ten-year-old heart, that was about as cool as things got. What a great way to describe life. "Hang in there, baby!" Now that's what I called living! A true motto I could stand on.

But let's face it, what did I know about life? I certainly had no idea what it meant to just "hang in there, baby."

I was privileged to be born into a good home. My parents were Christians, as were both my sisters. My sister Rhonda was six years older than me, and my oldest sister Mary Lu was six years older than her. Our godly grandmother completed our little clan, and I'm grateful for the years she lived in our home.

As you can probably tell, I was perfectly situated on the family tree. Yes, I indeed was the baby of the family. Everyone watched out for Lynn and that suited me just fine. It was natural to let others take care of me. Life was simple, predictable, and familiar.

So what on earth did I know about those words, "Hang in there. baby"?

Growing up in the Baptist church, I was well aware that God loved me and that I loved Him. Attending Sunday school, vacation Bible school, junior choir, and of course *two* services every Sunday was about as normal to me as breathing. I fondly remember a children's service where a lovely lady shared the gospel. Her stylish clothing and long hair were the first things to be noticed by my blossoming seven-year-old fashion sense. I sat quietly and listened to her speak about the death, burial, and resurrection of Jesus. I had heard all of this before and could even recite John 3:16.

But this time it was different. This was about having a relationship with God.

For by grace are ye saved through faith; and that not of yourselves: it is the gift of God: not of works, lest any man should boast. (Ephesians 2:8–9)

It all came together. God sent His Son Jesus to take what I deserved, so I could receive the gift. That day I surrendered my life, repented of my sin, and entered into a true relationship with God. Am I perfect? Not a bit, but I am saved, forgiven, and heaven-bound.

Wow! That was the most important day in my life.

As the years flew by, my life unfolded very much as I had hoped it would. I married John in 1985. He is one of the finest Christian men I have ever met. His faith and passion for God's Word gave me a sense of security and feeling of destiny. Marriage agreed with me, and I thanked God for His grace upon our lives.

Often I wondered if we would one day be used in full time ministry… but that's a whole other chapter.

Two years later, our daughter Katie was born. She was and continues to be a to-the-book kind of girl. My pregnancy was typical and her birth went exactly how the prenatal classes described. She brought joy to our lives and happiness to our home.

Looking back, I guess I was pretty smug in those days. Little Miss Perfect. Ugh! Once again, I definitely had no idea what it meant to "hang in there, baby."

Five years after Katie was born, our little family suffered the heartache of a miscarriage. Eleven weeks into the pregnancy, I was hospitalized and subsequently informed that I had lost the baby. It hurt to tell Katie that she was no longer awaiting a little brother or sister.

Pride pinched my heart. Why would this happen to my picture-perfect family? After all, in my opinion, we were doing everything right.

A number of months passed before I was expecting once again. This pregnancy was miserable. Round-the-clock morning sickness, fainting, and exhaustion seemed to plague me. Unlike my labour with Katie, this birth was difficult.

Nonetheless, a nine-pound-fifteen-ounce baby boy was placed in my arms on a cold January morning. Benjamin David Dunham completed our little family. John and I had a daughter and a son. It all looked so perfect.

As the months passed, Ben wasn't reaching any of the milestones we so eagerly anticipated. Rather than forming language, he would scream. He seemed to scream all day and most decidedly all night. He fixated on objects and often threw things in fits of rage.

Our doctor began to show concern and I naturally began to panic. I prayed in my heart of hearts, begging God to fix whatever was wrong with my son.

However, things did not get better and our doctor informed us that Ben needed to see a specialist. I remember donning my

"Christian smile," thanking the doctor, and walking out the door. My makeup was perfect, my clothes stylish, and every hair on my head in place, but inside I was falling to pieces.

At that moment, Satan took his chance to taunt me. It wasn't audible, but it was ugly and cruel. I felt like a failure. But I stuffed the hurt down into my heart.

The good Christian girl who prided herself on having a scripture for any situation couldn't come up with a single reason as to why this was happening. This wasn't part of my master plan. My need to fix things tried to kick in, yet I only recall feeling tired and numb. My cakewalk through life was now entering the unknown.

Our family outings became consumed by sleepless nights, medication regimes, seemingly endless therapy sessions, numerous specialists, resources for exceptional children, and even a visit to a child psychiatrist. My head spun as I tried to "cure" Ben with flashcards and anything else I could get my hands on.

As you, my dear reader, have probably already figured out, Ben was diagnosed severely autistic. It has been close to three decades since John and I first heard those words. Though we are at peace with God's providence, the word *autism* still carries a sting. The condition is definitely more easily spoken about today, but in the 1990s our family was entering what felt like uncharted territory.

Years passed and Ben grew. Teenage milestones didn't mean much to me since Ben was assessed to have arrested at the cognitive age of two, and to this day he has remained pretty much the same. Physically, he towered over both John and myself, though, and as a teenager his aggressive behaviour skyrocketed. When not self-harming, he would attack me. Many times I would enter the doctor's office covered with bites, bruises, and scratches—which led to more doctors, more medications, and more diagnoses. Severe autism, epic mood swings, profound learning disability, and anxiety all labelled my dear boy's life.

No one saw it, but my heart was breaking. Despite everything John, Katie, and I loved this child more than words could ever express. Moments of peace gave us glimmers of hope, but we walked on eggshells every day. I, Little Miss Sunday School, was starting to feel like the cat on that poster. I was *just* hanging in there, baby.

Friend, God's Word does not call us to "hang in there, baby." Rather we are called to *stand*. Ephesians 6:13 states, *"Wherefore take unto you the whole armour of God, that ye may be able to withstand in the evil day, and having done all, to stand."* That is what I want for you, and it's what I want for me—to stand in the day of trouble, not cower and claw like the cat in the poster, nor desperately cling to a weak and bending branch. Our security is found in Christ and Christ alone. When God says, *"I will never leave thee, nor forsake thee"* (Hebrews 13:5), He means it.

But will there be times when you feel alone? In short, yes.

The hymn writer Edward Mote explained it far better than I ever could:

When darkness veils his lovely face,
    I rest on his unchanging grace;
    in every high and stormy gale,
    my anchor holds within the veil.

His oath, his covenant, his blood,
    support me in the whelming flood;
    when all around my soul gives way,
    he then is all my hope and stay.

On Christ, the solid Rock, I stand:
    all other ground is sinking sand;
    all other ground is sinking sand.[1]

Those words were penned more than one hundred eighty years ago. Now there's a real motto for life!

REFLECTION

When you don't see God's plan, trust His character. When you feel alone, obey His Word. If you do, I promise you that He will prove Himself faithful.

My story is no more important than your story. Perhaps my perspective pales in comparison to all you've had to endure. I'm sharing my story simply because it's the only one I have.

It's my sincere prayer that the following collection of devotionals will encourage your heart. Each chapter will contain a personal narrative, a word of reflection, and verses of encouragement. Feel free to laugh with me, and by all means feel free to cry with me. There are no rules, no homework, and no certain days on which you have to read. Just consider this a grab-and-go book whenever you need a spiritual boost.

It is my deepest desire to motivate, stir, and spur you on to a closer relationship with God. And please share your story too! It's the only one you have.

Standing on the promises of Christ, my King,
    Through eternal ages let his praises ring;
    Glory in the highest, I will shout and sing,
    Standing on the promises of God.

Standing, standing,
    Standing on the promises of God, my Savior;

[1] Edward Mote, "My Hope Is Built on Nothing Less," 1834.

Standing, standing,
I'm standing on the promises of God.

Standing on the promises that cannot fail.
When the howling storms of doubt and fear assail,
By the living Word of God I shall prevail,
Standing on the promises of God.

Standing on the promises of Christ, the Lord,
Bound to him eternally by love's strong cord,
Overcoming daily with the Spirit's sword,
Standing on the promises of God.

Standing on the promises I cannot fall,
List'ning ev'ry moment to the Spirit's call,
Resting in my Savior as my all in all,
Standing on the promises of God.[2]

---

[2] Russell Kelso Carter, "Standing on the Promises of Christ My King," 1886.

And let us consider one another to provoke
unto love and to good works…
(Hebrews 10:24)

Wherefore comfort yourselves together, and
edify one another, even as also ye do.
(1 Thessalonians 5:11)

The Appointment

In short, I have a horrible sense of direction. For my driving test, I literally wrote an "L" on my left hand to help keep everything straight—kind of embarrassing since my husband was a driving examiner for eighteen years!

To this day, the words *left* or *right* can still plunge me into a cold sweat. You know that woman, hopelessly lost at the mall? Wave. It's probably me!

I recall the time Ben was to meet with a specialist at Toronto's SickKids hospital. Consultations tend to make me anxious, and when I feel anxious I become meticulous about details. What details? That's easy: deciding on everyone's outfits, of course! Twenty-five years later, I still remember precisely what I wore to that appointment.

Meanwhile, my practical husband consulted his maps. Yes, you heard me right. *Maps.* John is a stickler for maps and punctuality.

So at the very least we were going to arrive well dressed and on time. We make a good team!

The drive to Toronto was tense. Traffic was stop-and-go and it didn't help to know that Ben could go ballistic at any moment. Yet we arrived with time to spare. Parking was a challenge, but we accomplished it without incident. So far so good.

Entering the large atrium of the hospital, we were welcomed by cheerful decor and gleaming floors. John's duty was to keep Ben happy, and my role was to complete our paperwork registration at the front desk.

Despite my apprehension, I continued to trust that my master plan was working.

Then it happened: my life entered the twilight zone.

Upon keying Ben's name into the computer, the receptionist informed me that our appointment was at the Department of Neurology, located in a totally different building. She calmly explained that it was within walking distance of the main hospital.

I thought I was going to faint. So much for my brilliant attention to the details.

But I did what I always do. I donned my Christian smile and desperately tried not to look stunned. If that poor girl could have only heard my inner dialogue, though!

How could this be happening to us? We planned, we prepared, we even used maps! And now she's actually giving me, of all people, directions. Did she say one block and turn left, or was it one block and turn right? Was it the first building, or the second building? Am I going to have to cross any roads…?

My head spun with every word. I could have really used that "L" on my left hand right then… but at that point, it would have better belonged on my forehead.

Oblivious to our sudden change of plans, John was dutifully fulfilling his role: doing whatever it took to keep Ben calm.

Hopelessly I walked over and blurted out that we were in the wrong building.

And thus we found ourselves outside in the middle of Toronto, speedwalking, with a five-year-old autistic boy! At times I lost sight of John and Ben completely. Men in suits seemed to block my vision on every side. This appointment was literally two years in the making, and suddenly we found ourselves separated, lost, and ready to quit.

Amid the chaos, noise, and confusion, a man in a suit calmly called out, "John, what are you doing here?"

It was our friend Vic from our church in Whitby. In a city of more than two and a half million people, God had put a friend right in the centre of our path. Totally at ease, Vic knew exactly where the building was located. After a quick tutorial, we were on our way… and Vic simply blended back into the sea of well-dressed strangers.

Up the elevator and into the doctor's office we flew. Funnily enough, it was the doctor who was late, and we ended up sitting in the waiting room for close to an hour.

The appointment was informative, helpful, and loud… very, very loud. Despite my detailed planning, Ben completely and utterly freaked out. Embarrassing as our son's meltdown was, though, that day began a wonderful relationship between Ben and his new doctor. To think it may have never happened if God hadn't strategically placed a friend right in the middle of our need.

REFLECTION

We attempt to look the part, smile our smile, and blend into the crowd, but inside we're seeking direction. God sees you. God loves you. Perhaps He has even sent a friend to guide you along the way. When someone helps you, praise the Lord. When you help someone, praise the Lord. We're on this journey together and God is faithful.

In shady, green pastures, so rich and so sweet,
God leads His dear children along;
Where the water's cool flow bathes the weary one's
feet,
God leads His dear children along.

Some through the waters, some through the flood,
  Some through the fire, but all through the blood;
  Some through great sorrow, but God gives a song,
  In the night season and all the day long.

Sometimes on the mount where the sun shines so bright,
  God leads His dear children along;
  Sometimes in the valley, in darkest of night,
  God leads His dear children along.

Though sorrows befall us and evils oppose,
  God leads His dear children along;
  Through grace we can conquer, defeat all our foes,
  God leads His dear children along.

Away from the mire, and away from the clay,
  God leads His dear children along;
  Away up in glory, eternity's day,
  God leads His dear children along.[3]

---

[3] G.A. Young, "In Shady Pastures So Rich and So Sweet," 1903.

For if they fall, the one will lift up his
fellow: but woe to him that is alone when
he falleth; for he hath not another to
help him up.
(Ecclesiastes 4:10)

THE FENCE

My house is cute. Over a century old, white with black trim, it actually resembles a little barn. I admit that buying an older home comes with its obstacles, but I still appreciate its charm and warmth. Amidst plumbing jobs, furnace woes, and roof repairs, this house has become our home.

When we first moved in 2004, the backyard had no fence. This was problematic, since in the world of autism Ben had been labelled a "runner." With no perception of boundaries, a runner does just that; they run. Roads held no particular danger in his eyes, nor did he understand the consequence of reckless behaviour.

So there we were, with a major road at both ends of our street... and no fence.

Pricing out every option only led to one conclusion: fences are ridiculously expensive. With most of our finances thrown into the downpayment, things were tight.

As usual, panic began to grip my heart. My apprehension over venturing out with Ben made me feel inadequate. He was fast and, to coin a phrase, I run like a girl.

With my back up against the wall, I knew exactly what I needed to do: I would phone my friend Caroline. Surely she would listen and sympathize with my plight. After all, isn't that what true-blue friends are for, to agree with you on everything?

But Caroline would have no part of my pity party.

"Lynn, do you believe that God led you to this house?"

"Yes," I snapped. "But you don't understand. This is a safety issue. If Ben takes off, he could be hurt, or even worse…"

She dug in a little deeper. "Lynn, does God know that Ben needs a fence?"

At this point, I actually rolled my eyes. Sorry about that, Caroline.

Despite my snarky attitude, she kindly continued. "Lynn, if God brought you to this house, do you really believe He is going to leave you now? He already knows exactly what Ben needs."

I was not pleased. I wanted sympathy, but instead Caroline spoke the truth. I looked inward, but she pointed upward.

When the conversation ended, she reminded me, as she so often does, that God is faithful. And I agreed. I still desperately knew that I needed a fence, but I agreed.

Within that same month, our good friend Harold rolled his truck into our driveway. The trailer bed was laden with tools, wood, and equipment. Joined by an entourage of members of his farming community, Harold set to work. Hammers flew, nails were pounded, and within a week Ben had both a fence and a safe place to run.

When the dust had settled, Harold presented John with an itemized receipt. At the bottom of the bill were three words: "paid in full." To this very day, Harold and his lovely wife Mary Lynn are two of our very dearest friends.

It was just as Caroline had said: God is faithful.

Withstanding many storms and harsh winters, that beloved fence protected Ben for almost twenty years. Tired, weatherbeaten, and worn, one side of the fence was taken down in the summer of 2023. It was like saying goodbye to an old friend.

But God wasn't finished with us yet. Our neighbour Dave covered the cost of completely replacing the fence. We are so very grateful for his kindness and friendship as well.

Most assuredly, our family has never taken any of these blessings lightly. Special thanks go out to each person mentioned in this beautiful true story. God indeed is faithful.

REFLECTION

Much like Ben, we too are runners. Without thought of consequence or danger, we choose our path. With abandon, we run our own show.

Ben needed safety; he needed a fence. He received that gift… pain in full.

We need a Saviour; we need salvation. Jesus offers that gift… pain in full.

Be not dismayed whate'er betide,
God will take care of you;
Beneath his wings of love abide,
God will take care of you.

God will take care of you,
through ev'ry day, o'er all the way;
He will take care of you,
God will take care of you.

Through days of toil when heart doth fail,
God will take care of you;
When dangers fierce your path assail,
God will take care of you.
No matter what may be the test,
God will take care of you;
Lean, weary one, upon his breast,
God will take care of you.[4]

---

[4] "God Will Take Care of You," Civilla D. Martin, 1904.

For by grace are ye saved through faith; and
that not of yourselves: it is the gift of God:
not of works, lest any man should boast.
(Ephesians 2:8–9)

And it shall come to pass, that whosoever
shall call on the name of the
Lord shall be saved.
(Acts 2:21)

Did You Ever Have a Favourite Toy?

Long before Tickle Me Elmo, Furby, or even Cabbage Patch Kids, there was a doll that stood head and shoulders above the rest. Her name was Mrs. Beasley. This amicable-looking doll was one of the hottest marketed toys of Christmas 1971. Frantic parents, including my own mother, searched malls for this precious commodity.

Thus it happened that on December 25, at six years of age, I held in my arms a genuine Mrs. Beasley doll.

The phenomenon started with the television sitcom *Family Affair*. This wholesome show told the story of Uncle Bill, who was raising his brother's orphaned children, Cissy, Buffy, and Jody. Along with their butler, Mr. French, this newly formed family navigated life from a classy apartment in New York City. The little girl on the show was Buffy, and Buffy had a doll—you guessed it, Mrs. Beasley.

And so began the legacy dubbed TV's most famous doll. Donning adorable wire spectacles and a polka dot apron, Mrs. Beasley was more than a doll; she was a friend.

Not far from our house lived a little girl who also had a Mrs. Beasley. While her doll retained its fresh out-of-the-box appearance, we will just say that mine resembled more of an organic, homey look. With hair askew and a half missing eyebrow—nail polish remover, who knew?—she was still beautiful to me.

Together Mrs. Beasley and I shared the carefree days of childhood. And when my father had a tumour removed from his back, I squeezed her tight as I walked the stark white hospital corridor. We were inseparable.

But time is no respecter of youth, and slowly but gently Mrs. Beasley was pushed aside in favour of pretty dresses, nail polish, homework, and eventually boys. In a matter of a few years I was grown up, married, and buying dolls for my own little girl.

My brother-in-law Luke once asked me about whatever happened to my Mrs. Beasley. Strangely enough, I didn't have an answer. Was she in my parents' attic? Had she been donated? She had been my favourite doll, my precious Christmas memory… and all I could do now was shrug my shoulders.

That Christmas, Luke and my sister Rhonda gifted me a delicate, five-inch glass replica of Mrs. Beasley.

A few years later, my mother and sister Mary Lu found an original Mrs. Beasley online. What a surprise it was that Christmas when I was reunited with those twinkling blue eyes and that happy grin?

Every December, I hang my glass figurine and sit Mrs. Beasley the Second on a little chair beside my Christmas tree. It's a sweet memory.

Life is fragile. Getting caught up in our own agendas, we neglect simple moments. The business of the day replaces quiet time as busy schedules clutter our thoughts. Even religious piety can mimic a relationship with Jesus.

Mrs. Beasley serves as an allegory of how joy can slip away—unnoticed, neglected, and forgotten.

A few years ago, I spotted a man walking downtown. Weatherbeaten and dishevelled, I wondered what his story was. Then I read what was written on his tee shirt: "The Best Things in Life Aren't Things." Wow. That line said a multitude.

Protect your heart, guard your passions, and never lose sight of God's grace.

REFLECTION

These words penned by Robert Robinson in 1758, at the age of twenty-two, reveal much about the human spirit:

> Prone to wander, Lord, I feel it,
> prone to leave the God I love;
> here's my heart; O take and seal it;
> seal it for thy courts above.[5]

[5] "Come, Thou Fount of Every Blessing," Robert Robinson, 1758.

Set your affection on things above, not on
things on the earth.
(Colossians 3:2)

In my Father's house are many mansions: if
it were not so, I would have told you. I go
to prepare a place for you.
(John 14:2)

Thou wilt shew me the path of life: in thy
presence is fulness of joy; at thy right hand
there are pleasures for evermore.
(Psalms 16:11)

Let your conversation be without
covetousness; and be content with such
things as ye have: for he hath said, I will
never leave thee, nor forsake thee.
(Hebrews 13:5)

Therefore my heart is glad, and my glory
rejoiceth: my flesh also shall rest in hope.
(Psalms 16:9)

THE LITTLE BOY

Years ago, my daughter and I taught a Sunday school class together. The church we were attending wasn't large, so all the kids gathered in one room. Varied in age, grade level, and maturity, each child brought something special to the table. While some kids burst with enthusiasm, others were delighted to help in any way they could. Younger or older, shy or rambunctious, each student blessed our hearts.

Vividly, I recall the time I was to teach the story of Mary Magdalene washing the feet of Jesus. Call me old school, but I absolutely love visual aids. With kudos to my daughter and her obsession with thrift shops, we were fortunate enough to own an authentic alabaster trinket box. What a perfect way to explain the ointment that Mary broke open from her own alabaster box! Outfitted with pictures, snacks, and the special little box, we were more than ready that Sunday morning. Check, check, and doublecheck!

Ascending the stairs, the kids ran in excited for the time we would share together. High-fives out of the way, and songs sung, we settled into our Bible time. While emphasizing the fact that only Jesus could forgive Mary of her sinful life, I lifted the first picture. I detailed her bravery to enter a house of religious leaders and stressed how we too must keep our eyes focused only on the Lord. Point after point, these sweet boys and girls paid close attention to the truth of repentance, humility, and worship.

Then the moment arrived. With a flourish and dramatic gesturing, I threw forth my hand and presented the little alabaster box. Perceiving that my crew was totally on board, I detailed the expense of the ointment. I intensified my voice and informed my class how this once sinful woman broke the box open and poured out the costly perfume. In tears of adoration, Mary washed and anointed her Saviour's feet. I then closed with a picture of her drying His feet with her hair.

Feeling rather pleased with my teaching, I quizzed the boys and girls on their lesson.

"What was the woman's name?" I asked.

"Mary," a younger child answered.

"Where did she live?"

"In Bethany," said an older one in triumph.

Cognizant of how utterly overboard I had gone in describing the extravagant perfume, I called out the next question: "With what did Mary wash the feet of Jesus?"

A sweet little boy, no more than six years of age, raised his hand. Quivering with emotion, he choked out, "Her tears."

A reverent hush fell over the room. I looked at my daughter. She too was visibly moved.

"Yes," I softly responded. "You are correct."

My heart squeezed. I had carefully detailed the cost of the perfume, the attitude of the religious leaders, and the breaking of the alabaster box. However, the little boy had gone straight to the heart of Mary. He had seen her tears. Tears of regret and repentance. Tears of praise. Tears of worship.

He had seen her tears.

Reflection

Just as Jesus saw Mary's tears, He sees your tears. Mary anointed Jesus's feet in a symbolic preparation for His imminent death, burial, and resurrection. Our tears of repentance are wiped away through Christ's finished sacrifice alone. Have you knelt in surrender at the feet of Jesus? He loves you. He sees your tears.

> Just as I am, without one plea,
> but that thy blood was shed for me,
> and that thou bidd'st me come to thee,
> O Lamb of God, I come, I come.
>
> Just as I am, and waiting not
> to rid my soul of one dark blot,
> to thee, whose blood can cleanse each spot,
> O Lamb of God, I come, I come.
>
> Just as I am, though tossed about
> with many a conflict, many a doubt,
> fightings and fears within, without,
> O Lamb of God, I come, I come.
>
> Just as I am, thou wilt receive,
> wilt welcome, pardon, cleanse, relieve;
> because thy promise I believe,
> O Lamb of God, I come, I come.[6]

[6] Charlotte Elliott, "Just as I Am, Without One Plea," 1836.

And, behold, a woman in the city, which
was a sinner, when she knew that Jesus sat
at meat in the Pharisee's house, brought
an alabaster box of ointment, and stood at
his feet behind him weeping, and began to
wash his feet with tears, and did wipe them
with the hairs of her head, and kissed his
feet, and anointed them with the ointment.
(Luke 7:37–38)

THE WINDOW

Hands down, fall is my favourite season. Crisp breezes, brilliantly coloured leaves, the glow of my fireplace (even if it is electric), and cozy sweaters. Just thinking about it gives me a hankering for tea and apple crisp.

Fifteen autumns ago, I stood at my window. My husband and daughter were working and I was home alone with Ben. My son was bent on going outside. As previously noted, we are blessed to have a safe, fully fenced yard. So, with a locking system on the gate, I had the luxury of supervising Ben right from the kitchen window.

Considering it was a chilly day, I opted for him to wear a pair of mittens with his jacket. Behavioural cues and verbal expectations out of the way, I felt reasonably assured that this little activity was going to go well.

I listened to music, keeping a watchful eye from my kitchen window. Clouds covered the sky with a haze as I mused whether rain would be in the forecast. Upon my phone ringing, I began a pleasant conversation with my sister.

Then it happened. Without warning, life took an unexpected turn. Without any apparent trigger, Ben bounded up the back stairs. In nothing short of a fit of rage, his fist smashed against the window. Being a century-old home, the brittle glass shattered everywhere.

Jumping back from shock, I can only describe the moment as being like a scene from an old western. I slammed down the phone, gathered my bearings, and darted out the door.

Frantically I searched my child for any sign of blood or injury. Miracle number one: his mittens had shielded him from even as much as a scratch.

Still horrified, I very loudly ordered him to go to his room. Miracle number two: Ben actually obeyed and ran to his room.

Frustrated and alone, I sank to the floor. I long to say that I was smiling my Christian smile. At the very least, I could have folded my hands and thanked God that no one was hurt. Rather, to my shame, I leaned against the oven door and cried my eyes out.

With messy mascara smeared over my face, I then uttered the two words I thought I would never say: "Why me?" There I sat before the God of the universe, having the absolute gall to ask, "Why me?"

Looking back, I realize that it wasn't just about the window. Sleep deprivation, juggling medications, going to endless doctor appointments, plastering holes in the walls, and explaining my life to what felt like every Tom, Dick, and Harry felt so… *daily*. It wasn't even the first window Ben had broken, but it was definitely the largest.

"Why me?" I had strived to serve God my whole life. I loved the Lord more than anyone or anything. At one time, I had even been willing to go to the mission field! Now I simply felt weak and insufficient.

"Why John?" Anyone who has met my husband would agree that he is warm-hearted and kind. This guy makes friends just standing in the lineup at the grocery store. He's true blue. I've witnessed him live out his faith consistently with a heart that follows after God.

"Why Katie?" Meek and uncomplaining, my daughter grew up in a home centred around her brother's needs. By the time she was eight, vacations were cancelled, restaurant trips rare, and every outing came accompanied by Plan A and Plan B.

"Why Ben?" My son lives in a confused, often frightening world. The slightest transitions can hurl him into hysterics. Shifting from laughing to crying, his emotions are raw and unpredictable. His verbal limitations incite meltdowns and often aggressive behaviour. Daily we pray for him to just have a good day.

Our family loves Ben with all our hearts, yet not one of us has ever received a hug from him.

That day, my thoughts were blurred, irrational, and disjointed. Coming from a mother's heart, these were groanings only Jesus could understand.

I was a mess and frankly I didn't care. Yet undeserving as I was, the Lord never left my side. He didn't zap me off the planet. He just loved me.

Do you recall that I mentioned there was music in my kitchen that afternoon? The noise of life ebbed as the song seemed to get just a little louder. The lyrics of "His Strength Is Perfect" by Steven Curtis Chapman sank deeply into my soul and I felt peace.

The answer was evident. God loved me. He loved John. He loved Katie. And most assuredly God loved Ben.

Wiping my tears, I stood back up, cleaned the mess, and taped cardboard over the window. In the next few days, the window was replaced. Life continued, but I was different. In my weakness, I had an advocate—and His strength is perfect.

All the way my Savior leads me.
What have I to ask beside?
Can I doubt his tender mercy,
Who thru' life has been my Guide?
Heav'nly peace, divinest comfort,
Here by faith in him to dwell!

For I know, whate'er befall me,
Jesus doeth all things well.

All the way my Savior leads me,
Cheers each winding path I tread;
Gives me grace for ev'ry trial,
Feeds me with the living Bread.
Tho' my weary steps may falter,
And my soul athirst may be,
Gushing from the Rock before me,
Lo! A spring of joy I see.

All the way my Savior leads me;
Oh, the fullness of His love!
Perfect rest to me is promised
In my Father's house above.
When my spirit, cloth'd immortal,
Wings its flight to realms of day
This my song thru' endless ages:
Jesus led me all the way.[7]

REFLECTION

Does the trial ahead seem more than you can bear? I get it. Difficulties don't simply vanish away just because we love God. Whether short-term, chronic, or right out of the blue, challenges do just that: they challenge you.

Earnestly and deeply lean into Jesus. He knows when the smile is fake and sees when the tears are real. Be encouraged that you are held in His mighty hand. He loves you.

---

[7] Fanny Crosby, "All the Way My Savior Leads Me," 1875.

Likewise the Spirit also helpeth our
infirmities: for we know not what we should
pray for as we ought: but the Spirit itself
maketh intercession for us with groanings
which cannot be uttered.
(Romans 8:26)

My brethren, count it all joy when ye fall
into divers temptations; knowing this, that
the trying of your faith worketh patience.
But let patience have her perfect work, that
ye may be perfect and entire,
wanting nothing.
(James 1:2–4)

The Reunion of a Lifetime

Decorations, twinkling lights, singing carols… I love it all! My holiday shopping starts in February and my tree is up by mid-November. If that's not irritating enough, I literally play Christmas music all year round. What can I say, I'm a Christmas nut!

Enter stage left: the year 2020. COVID-19 turned our world pretty much upside-down. With hospitals at capacity, jobs halted, and church doors locked, it all seemed like a weird dream.

By the time December rolled around, parades were cancelled, gatherings were limited, and in an odd way hand sanitizer became our new best friend. There we stood in long lineups for groceries, and of course toilet paper… who could ever forget the drama around the toilet paper?

Despite it all, Christmas came and it came just the same! 2020 may have looked different, but it definitely made a mark on all our lives. We could still echo the wise words of Tiny Tim: "God bless us everyone!"

Guilty as charged. I love Christmas movies too!

Enter stage right: Christmas 2021. Protocols still had to be observed and masks were still required, but life began to take on a little more wiggle room, enough at least for the ladies at my church to have a Christmas tea. Chairs would be socially distanced and masks worn, but we could do it together, which made everything good!

On the eve of the tea, those serving as hostesses gathered to decorate and prepare our tables. What a sweet time we shared. Laughter filled the room as the centrepieces were poised to perfection. And with the last cup and saucer neatly placed, the auditorium glowed with the splendour of the yuletide season.

Stepping back to admire our handiwork, my daughter and I could at last justify all our trips to the local dollar store.

Right about that time, our dear friend Sandy popped by for a wee chat. Smiling her bright smile, Sandy has a unique way of lighting up a room. She was stylishly dressed, rocking her fabulous haircut and elegant jewellery. Hair, clothes, and jewellery aside, Sandy is best known for having a heart of pure gold. Gracious and kind, her life serves as an example of godly wisdom.

Scanning the placards on my table, Sandy commented that she knew one of my guests from her years as a teacher at R.A. Hutchison. My eyebrows raised. I had been a student of that very school in the 1970s. Curious of anyone we might have in common, the very first name to pop out of my mouth was that of my sweet kindergarten teacher.

Without a moment of hesitation, Sandy exclaimed, "That's me!"

So much for social distancing. Without hesitation, I threw my arms around the very person I had idolized when I was a child! Gasps of laughter punctuated our conversation, while I repeated "I can't believe this!" and "Who would have ever imagined?" in rapid succession.

Upon hearing my maiden name, Sandy not only recalled me as a child but accurately pinpointed that I had been one of her "morning" students.

Before the evening was over, we had told our wild reunion story to pretty much every person in that room.

The following day, Sandy arrived at the party with a guest. There to greet me was my first-grade teacher. How much more could my poor heart take? Here I was, a plain nondescript kid, conversing with two of my childhood heroes. The fictional details of a movie deal swirled around in my head; we could entitle it *The Christmas Tea-chers*.

You can't make this stuff up, folks! My very cool kindergarten teacher with her groovy clothes and far-out jewellery turned out to be the same classy person I had known for so many years simply as Sandy, a woman who in times past had ministered alongside me at the nursing home and attended the very same church as me. And she had taught me my ABCs!

You may be thinking, "Surely the two of you should have recognized each other years ago." First of all, Sandy looks far too young to have ever been my teacher. Second, she seemed so tall to my five-year-old eyes, and now I towered over her. Third, she had a different last name and hair colour. Come to think of it, I had a different last name and hair colour too!

Ultimately, God in His providence held out this precious reunion gift, not to be opened until, Christmas 2021.

REFLECTION

We all long for that picture-perfect holiday, with meticulous homes, perfect decor, and the faint scent of cinnamon. Yet life happens, flour gets spilled on the floor, and tinfoil pans collapse, pouring turkey grease everywhere.

Yes, those things have happened to me.

Jesus's birth didn't happen so we could have a really cool holiday. He came into our world because we needed a Saviour. Just imagine: perfection coming to the earth, dying in our place, and rising from the grave—and one day He will return for His own.

Are you prepared? Talk about a reunion! No one knows when that day will occur, but be assured that it will be the reunion of a lifetime!

> Savior, like a shepherd lead us,
> Much we need Thy tender care;
> In Thy pleasant pastures feed us,
> For our use Thy folds prepare:
> Blessèd Jesus, blessèd Jesus,
> Thou hast bought us, Thine we are;
> Blessèd Jesus, blessèd Jesus,
> Thou hast bought us, Thine we are.[8]

---

[8] Dorothy A. Thrupp and Henry F. Lyte, "Savior, Like a Shepherd Lead Us," 1836.

For the Lord himself shall descend from
heaven with a shout, with the voice of the
archangel, and with the trump of God: and
the dead in Christ shall rise first: then we
which are alive and remain shall be caught
up together with them in the clouds, to
meet the Lord in the air: and so shall we
ever be with the Lord.
(1 Thessalonians 4:16–17)

Rejoice evermore.
(1 Thessalonians 5:16)

This is the day which the Lord hath made;
we will rejoice and be glad in it.
(Psalms 118:24)

Listening for a Calling

From a young age, I have held great respect for people who devote their lives to full-time Christian service. Missionary stories always gripped my imagination, and pastor's wives were revered in my eyes.

Is it any surprise that my dolls would hop in their psychedelic trailer and travel around as gospel singers? Many a Sunday afternoon I would sit at the organ, thankfully turned off, and testify to an empty living room of the Lord's strength to get me through the trials of life. I was roughly eight years old at the time, so you can only imagine how soul-stirring that scene must have been. Yet I had been poised and primed to go into all the world and preach the gospel!

Finally, that glorious day arrived. My Aunt Lois gave me a plethora of her old Sunday school flannelgraphs. If I hadn't been ready to fulfill the great commission before, I was prepared now!

Armed with a yellow suitcase of songbooks and flannelgraphs I headed to the uncharted mission field of my front yard. The boy next door, Sean, was—and continues to be—like a brother to me. He was Catholic and I was Baptist, and together we were going to win the neighbourhood for the Lord.

Anticipating that some unsuspecting friend would stop and listen, I dramatically flung the Bible characters onto a flannel bedsheet as Sean led singing from illustrated songbooks. A couple of times, we actually nabbed a kid long enough to present the story of the prodigal son and literally tell them to pray the sinner's prayer.

In retrospect, it's a wonder that kids weren't running in every direction when they saw me swinging my yellow suitcase. Come to think of it, they probably were!

During my teenage years, I became more serious about the Lord's direction in my life. Reading biographies of faithful saints spurred me on to a higher calling. I joined a youth group where we went to the mall and asked other teens if they would go to heaven were they to die that very day. Although somewhat heavy-handed, it opened many a dialogue where peers actually did want to talk about God, life, and eternity.

Grateful for those opportunities, I most certainly was taught the truth of 1 Peter 3:15: *"be ready always to give an answer to every man that asketh you a reason of the hope that is in you with meekness and fear…"*

Celebrating the arrival of marriage, my husband John and I eagerly discussed the possibility of full-time ministry. As a team, we led a college and career group, taught Sunday school, held monthly services at a nursing home, and enjoyed musical opportunities along the way. Visiting different churches, I would perform ventriloquism while John presented the gospel through "chalk talks."

The very desires of our hearts were being fulfilled, yet we continued to look for the grander picture.

Attending missionary conferences, John and I wanted nothing less than to be used by the Lord. This is kind of embarrassing, but when missionaries spoke about faraway lands I actually sat there and calculated how much hair dye I would have to pack in my little missionary trunk to get through two years of service. Is it any wonder that the Lord never called me to be a missionary?

Years came and went, our children were born, and we continued to serve in the local church. All too soon, Ben's autism pretty much turned our world upside-down. Navigating our new normal, my overly romanticized view of ministry took on more of a "hang in there, baby" narrative.

I grew older. In what has felt like a blink of an eye, my sixties have now appeared on the horizon. The big missionary journey never did happen. There were no fond farewells, no waving my hankie to friends and family, no missionary letters written and no missionary letters read.

Yet hopefully a bit of wisdom has come with age. In hindsight, every opportunity to serve the Lord has been a fulfillment of the desires of my heart. Singing, telling my story to ladies groups, ventriloquism, and teaching Sunday School have all been part of the greater picture—not across the seas, nor even to faraway places, but right where I lived, worked, and played.

Life didn't go according to my plan, but rather the Father's plan. In opposition to my hoarded resources, God's faithfulness has shone in my weakness. Vulnerability has allowed John and me to minister with an understanding spirit. Slowly I've realized that it's all about Jesus and not me.

No, life didn't turn out the way I expected, but I do hope that the bumpy road has made me kinder and gentler.

One day, with an extremely heavy heart, I questioned my husband about why it was that we never were placed in true full-time Christian service. Sharing the ache of my heart, John whispered, "We were. We were placed in ministry… to our son."

To this day, I hold in highest regard those who devote their lives to the Lord's work. May God bless the pastors and their wives who give so unselfishly of their family, time, and resources. May God bless our missionaries who leave hearth and home to spread the gospel to faraway places. And may God bless those who minister right where we live, work, and play.

REFLECTION

Wherever God tells you to go, go. Whoever He tells you to talk with, talk. Whatever He wants you to do, do it. As the old saying goes, "Bloom where you are planted!" Follow the words of this hymn written in 1896 and you will never go wrong:

1 All to Jesus I surrender,
    All to Him I freely give;
    I will ever love and trust Him,
    In His presence daily live.

I surrender all, I surrender all;
    All to Thee, my blessed Savior,
    I surrender all.[9]

---

[9] Judson W. Van DeVanter, "I Surrender All," 1896.

Delight thyself also in the Lord: and he shall
give thee the desires of thine heart.
(Psalms 37:4)

For I know the thoughts that I think toward
you, saith the Lord, thoughts of peace, and
not of evil, to give you an expected end.
(Jeremiah 29:11)

Trust in the Lord with all thine heart; and
lean not unto thine own understanding. In
all thy ways acknowledge him, and he shall
direct thy paths.
(Proverbs 3:5–6)

The Blessing of Groceries

Children hear far more than we often realize. I didn't fully comprehend this truth until my daughter was roughly eight years of age.

My neighbour at the complex where we were living at the time dropped in for a visit. We had become good friends over the years, and this happened during this chapter in our lives that I was blessed to see her come to know the Lord as her Saviour. John and I often had her and her husband over for Bible studies. Their zeal to unpack scriptural truth remains a precious memory.

With my daughter busy doing schoolwork in the kitchen, my neighbour and I settled ourselves in the living room for a wee chat. Not once thinking that Katie would overhear our conversation, my friend poured out her heart. She had three teenagers and a grandchild all under her roof and grocery shopping was proving to be a challenge. Her husband was out of work and stressed with health issues.

We didn't talk long, but afterward she seemed a little less burdened to have had a sympathetic ear to listen and care.

Prepared to return home, my friend stood up to leave. At that stage, Katie entered the living room dragging a large shopping bag. With a huge smile on her face, she presented the sack. Mutually gasping, we realized that Katie had completely emptied the refrigerator freezer. Chicken, porkchops, a roast, frozen vegetables… you name it, it was bundled and ready to go.

Nervously laughing, my neighbour explained to my little girl that she was not to worry about what she had heard. Katie didn't say a word, so once again the neighbour assured her that although her kindness was appreciated, it was probably best if she should put the groceries back in Mommy's freezer.

Watching this series of events unfold, God impressed upon my heart the importance of compassion and humility—compassion for this family I knew was struggling, and humility in grasping that my eight-year-old would be sensitive enough to stand in the gap.

Silently, as not to embarrass anyone, I nodded my head and gently asked my friend to please take the groceries. With tears brimming in her eyes, she thanked Katie and reverently took the gift.

Standing at my screen door, I watched the woman carry home more than just a bag of frozen food; she also carried a simple story of God providing for her family through, of all people, the little girl across the road.

I didn't chide my daughter for emptying the freezer, nor did I gush to her about what an unselfish person she had been. We continued our afternoon as though what had happened was as normal as breathing.

Little did I know that I had been given a glimpse into the future.

My daughter, now in her thirties, grew into one of the most selfless people I know. Humble and quiet-spirited, she would happily give someone in need the shirt off her back. When a crisis presents itself, she sets forth a practical way to help meet that need. Encouraging people with small but thoughtful gifts gives her joy.

And as a footnote to this story, one of Katie's favourite things to do is surprise me personally with bags of groceries… delivered with a smile.

REFLECTION

Do you have a gift you want used for the glory of God? With the faith and humility of a child, seek His direction and rise to the challenge. A small kindness may not seem earth-shattering in your eyes, but a word, act, or deed given in obedience to the Saviour might turn out to be a cherished chapter in someone else's story.

> When He cometh, when He cometh
> To make up His jewels,
> All His jewels, precious jewels,
> His loved and His own:
>
> Like the stars of the morning,
> His bright crown adorning,
> They shall shine in their beauty,
> Bright gems for His crown.
>
> He will gather, He will gather
> The gems for His kingdom;
> All the pure ones, all the bright ones,
> His loved and His own.
>
> Little children, little children,
> Who love their Redeemer,
> Are the jewels, precious jewels,
> His loved and His own.[10]

---

[10] William Cushing, "When He Cometh, When He Cometh," 1856.

Having then gifts differing according
to the grace that is given to us, whether
prophecy, let us prophesy according to
the proportion of faith; or ministry, let
us wait on our ministering: or he that
teacheth, on teaching; or he that exhorteth,
on exhortation: he that giveth, let him
do it with simplicity; he that ruleth,
with diligence; he that sheweth mercy,
with cheerfulness. Let love be without
dissimulation. Abhor that which is evil;
cleave to that which is good.
(Romans 12:6–9)

And whatsoever ye do in word or deed, do
all in the name of the Lord Jesus, giving
thanks to God and the Father by him.
(Colossians 3:17)

The Rulebook

My home thrives on rules, so many rules that I can barely name them all. There are specific times of day when lights are to be turned on—and just as important, times when lights are to be turned off. There are rules governing dietary specifications, medication regimes, bedtime logistics, how loud we speak, washroom schedules, and music selections. Other rules govern our daily drives and who takes them, the operation of white noise machines at night, who attends church and who stays home, and even what time of day the dehumidifier should run. (Between five o'clock and nine-thirty, in case you're wondering.)

No, I'm not a weirdo legalist, nor am I a control freak ready to pounce on anyone who doesn't toe the line. Simply put, I'm the mom of a severely autistic, anxiety-plagued, obsessive-compulsive adult son. Whether I find it convenient or not, he navigates life through familiarity and rigid schedules.

I would love to say that this isn't as bad as it sounds, but in all sincerity it can be pretty irritating. When Ben's routine is interrupted, life gets unpleasant. Schedule interferences, simple transitions, or heaven forbid a baby's cry can trigger anything from screaming to headbanging—or worst of all, an epic meltdown.

Why expose the unpleasant side of life? I do so because for too many years I burdened myself with the stigma of needing to look perfect. After all, shouldn't a good Christian home be just that—perfect?

The older I grow, the more I come to realize that life doesn't always play by the rules. My normal is different than I expected when I was younger. And if you've been curious enough to stick with me to this point, my guess is that your normal isn't what you expected either.

Difficulties come in all shapes and sizes. Caring for someone is just as heavy as finding yourself in the vulnerable place of needing someone to care for you. I'm not a professional counsellor, nor do I pretend to be one, but I do have the experience of three decades of full-time caregiving. I trust that what I've gleaned along my journey will give a little peace to your weary soul.

To the caregiver, you are not alone. Isolationism and discouragement create a pit that you can easily fall into, especially when you're tired. Overcompensating in order to look like you have it all together is not your burden to bear. Allow yourself the dignity to share what you're comfortable sharing—and when well-meaning people step over the line, learn to smile and steer the conversation in a different direction.

It's one thing to aid someone in understanding your situation and another to tear the scab off your soul every time you walk out the door. There's nothing wrong with just wanting to have a friend who can belly-laugh with you over an otherwise crazy day. Other times, a trusted confidant can grant you the vulnerability to share your heart, or just celebrate what others may consider a minor accomplishment.

In my family, each of us is blessed to be part of a small life group Bible study with our church. It takes some scheduling on our part, but the investment in spiritual maintenance is well worth the effort.

Special shoutout to the ladies of my Wednesday morning Bridge Whitby Bible study! You encourage me more than you will ever know.

On days that are long, and nights that are longer, you may feel like you have nothing more to give. I get it, believe me. I really do get it. Unfortunately, in those times it's easy to snap at people or believe the lie that the rest of the world is floating by on a cloud. Take it from this old gal: the spiral into self-pity isn't at all attractive.

So what is our takeaway? Putting it plainly, don't settle for a depressive lifestyle. Your narrative may be different than the one you would have chosen, but it is unique and holds purpose. Hold tight to Jesus, lean into the cross, and refuse to permit despair to wipe out your ability to minister grace. It may sound trite, but God's grace is exactly as lovely as the word itself: *grace*. We need grace to wipe away the tears, grace to keep on keeping on, and grace to know when to throw on some lipstick and allow yourself to smile.

For those who seek to encourage caregivers, I don't wish to sound harsh, but unless you are a doctor please don't pretend to be one. When you bombard someone who is honestly following a medical support system, your two cents can often feel overwhelming and judgmental.

When Ben was young I would visit his specialist, burdened by all the things people were telling me I should do to "fix" my son. Being a no-nonsense professional, she dryly replied, "Lynn, my husband is a lawyer, and he would tell you, 'Free advice is worth exactly what you pay for it.'" Processing those words gave me a sense of security to trust Ben's medical team and be gracious to those who push boundaries.

My point is that we should encourage those who need a kind word. We should bless them, pray for them, or even send a note or help with a meal. But please leave the medical care to the professionals. Hugs and understanding go further than you will ever imagine. Your friend loves their special family member every bit as much as you love the members of your own family.

In short, follow the golden rule.

Whether caregiving or receiving care, spiritual renewal is paramount. I admit that when days are weary and life chaotic, my Bible time doesn't look the way I wish it did. Instead of opening my Bible with a cup of tea and fistful of brightly coloured neon highlighters, I take in scriptural teaching via my earbuds.

When the way is rough, my prayers might only consist of four words: "Please, please help me." Whatever your lot may be, God really does see you, hear you, and most of all love you.

True, my house is navigated by rules. Is it ever spontaneous? Not on your life. Fun? Well, we certainly have learned to laugh over something as bizarre as flour being thrown around the kitchen… only to have it shoot out the back of the vacuum when we attempted to clean up the mess.

I well remember the day we celebrated the completion of my son's toilet training. He was ten. Our doctor was ecstatic and my friend Caroline broke down in tears of joy.

Yes, we have learned to celebrate amidst the storm. Small accomplishments, dear friends, unexpected blessings, and happy moments are all glimpses of sweet grace.

REFLECTION

A number of years ago, I bitterly griped to my sister, Mary Lu, that my son's love was conditioned on whether or not his rules were being followed. Wise as always, she counselled me, "Lynn, Ben has taught you about unconditional love—for he has taught you to give it."

That, my friend, is exactly what I needed to hear. We scheme, complain, and even offer God suggestions on how He might "fix" our problems. In layman's terms, we want Him to follow our rules.

Surpassing our list of shallow demands, Jesus offers us something better. He offers us peace of the heart, rest for our souls, and always sweet grace.

Day by day, God's gracious love surrounds me
As a balm to soothe my troubled heart.
Countless cares and worries that confound me
Fade away or quietly depart,
For His heart is kind beyond all measure,
And He comforts us as He knows best.
Ev'ry day, with all its pain and pleasure,
Mingles tears with peace and rest.

Day by day, the Lord is ever near me,
Granting loving mercies for each hour,
And my care He gladly bears, and cheers me
With His counsel pure and holy pow'r.
I'll not fear for what may come tomorrow,
Though the path ahead I cannot see.
He assures that in all joy or sorrow,
"As thy days, thy strength shall be."

Help me rest in quiet consolation.
Help me trust Thy promises, O Lord.
When I'm faced with daily tribulation,
Help me find the strength to live Thy word.
Then, dear Lord, when toil and trouble find me,
Hold me steadfast in Thy pow'rful hand.
Day by day, Thy strength will bear me kindly
Till I reach the promised land.[11]

---

[11] Carolina Sandell (author), A.K. Skoog (translation), "Day by Day," 1865.

Come unto me, all ye that labour and are
heavy laden, and I will give you rest. Take
my yoke upon you, and learn of me; for I
am meek and lowly in heart: and ye shall
find rest unto your souls.
(Matthew 11:28–29)

But I have trusted in thy mercy; my heart
shall rejoice in thy salvation.
(Psalms 13:5)

THE GOOD

My friend Lynne (with an *e*) embodies the gift of hospitality. I have personally witnessed her organize everything from funerals to New Year's Eve parties.

Amazingly, it's been almost forty years now since Lynne and her husband Don masterfully catered my very own wedding reception. Capable and efficient, Lynne can feed a crowd, iron a stack of tablecloths, tackle a crisis, and decorate for a party without breaking as much as a sweat. When others would be freaked out by an unexpected crowd, Lynne embraces the drama and simply whips up "just one more" loaf of sandwiches.

Year after year, Lynne and Don plunge themselves into a month-long Christmas-decorating extravaganza. With a myriad of labelled totes and countless strands of garland, they transform their home into a cozy winter hideaway. By December 1, no doubt every room in their house looks like a shot from a Christmas magazine. With lights hung and candles glowing, most assuredly a mug of hot apple cider awaits you in their kitchen.

In addition to the interior charm, the outside of their home boasts glittering lights that lead to Don's workshop. If you're picturing a sprawling property in the country, you couldn't be more mistaken. The scene I'm describing is that of a modest semi-detached home in an average neighbourhood in the same city where I live.

Don, Lynne, and their special daughter Cathy, have more than a house; they have a home. A home where people are cherished and Christ is honoured.

Too many times to count, I have been the recipient of homemade goodies from Lynne, not to mention a baking lesson or two.

A particular occasion is fondly etched in my memory. As I often had before, I had been invited over for a cup of tea. Wearing jeans and a T-shirt, I was surprised to be welcomed by a coffee table laden with Lynne's finest china. You wouldn't find a lovelier spread at Balmoral Castle. Dainty treats, cheese, and sliced fruit all awaited me.

I was humbled yet inquisitive as to why such finery had been prepared for none other than plain ol' me. Call me wacky, but before that day I had been clueless that napkins even existed to perfectly match china patterns. What would they think of next?

In a no-fuss, straightforward tone, Lynne explained her choice of decor. After years of collecting exquisite dishware, she confessed that it was only ever used for "good" or "special" occasions. Yet that week it had dawned on her that any time spent with friends was just that; it was good. What could be more special than friendship, comfortable conversations, pleasant memories, and honest laughter?

Our time was warm and our fellowship sweet, but more than that… it was *good*.

REFLECTION

God's gifts are good. Amidst the conflict and pressures of life, pause, sip a cup of coffee, giggle over a happy memory, slide off your shoes, and take the time to thank God for the *good*.

Bless this house, O Lord we pray,
Make it safe by night and day.
Bless these walls so firm and stout,
Keeping want and trouble out.
Bless the roof and chimneys tall,
Let thy peace lie overall.
Bless this door that it may prove,
Ever open to joy and love.

Bless these windows shining bright,
Letting in God's Heavenly light,
Bless the hearth, ablazing there,
With smoke ascending like a prayer!
Bless the people here within,
Keep them pure and free from sin.
Bless us all that we may be,
Fit O Lord to dwell with thee.
Bless us all that one day we may dwell,
O Lord! With Thee![12]

---

[12] Helen Taylor, "Bless This House," 1927.

Every good gift and every perfect gift is from
above, and cometh down from the Father of
lights, with whom is no variableness, neither
shadow of turning.
(James 1:17)

Therefore all things whatsoever ye would
that men should do to you, do ye even so to
them: for this is the law and the prophets.
(Matthew 7:12)

GRACE IN THE UNEXPLAINED

We are not getting out of this.

That was my last thought before the airbag exploded in my face.

Awaking to the tearful sound of my husband praying, I found myself lying on the side of a country road. My head pounded like a gong as John whispered that we had been in a bad accident. Eight-year-old Katie silently clung to her dad and Ben's signature scream reminded us that we were definitely not in heaven.

It was the third day of the last vacation our family was ever going to take. That summer of 1996 took us on an unexpected journey.

Airborne, our tiny purple economy car had veered into a ditch and straight into a brick culvert. As the interior billowed with black smoke, my husband panicked. Aided by some good Samaritans, though, Katie and Ben were pulled to safety through the hatchback trunk. John then managed to pry the passenger door open, dreading the worst. I was completely unresponsive and bleeding heavily from above my right eye when he dragged me to the side of the road.

Witnesses gathered, pointing wildly in the direction where the reckless driver who had caused the action—he was indeed later caught and charged—had fled. As blaring sirens sent my son into hysterics, I felt the EMTs gently strap me onto a board. My husband explained to the paramedic that we were from Ajax and only renting a cottage in Prince Edward County.

Oddly willing myself to figure out what in the world a cottage was, I muttered, "Are the kids okay?"

John held my hand and tearfully answered in the affirmative.

Once in the emergency room, he juggled Ben in his arms. Katie, as always, was easy to handle, but with our son's unpredictability it was best not to let his feet touch the floor. Securing the use of a hospital phone, my husband dialled the only number he knew could be of immediate help: my eighty-four-year-old grandmother who lived in Picton.

Yes, you did read that correctly. Eighty-four years old.

As my concussion was being assessed, I felt a needle being injected above my right eye. Amidst the bright lights, stitches, and loud noises, a kerfuffle took place by the swinging ER doors.

"Ma'am, this is an emergency area. You will need to take a seat in the waiting room. Ma'am, ma'am, I said you will need to take a—"

"Excuse me, but my granddaughter is in that room and her husband needs me."

My feisty grandmother Rose was undeterred as she swished her no-nonsense English pride into the examination room. Met by John's tears and hugs, she immediately took on the role of chief caregiver. She watched over the children, including Ben and all his issues, until my parents arrived almost two hours later. She never wavered. Now in heaven, I think of what a grand lady she really was!

Admitted to a hospital room, I threw up into a metal dish. My face hurt almost as much as the gong that was banging in my head.

"What do I look like?" I groggily asked my husband once I was medicated.

"Beautiful."

Considering that the camera never lies—and believe me, there are photos—I was thankful for his reply.

The severe facial "rug burn" I'd sustained via the airbag was now accented by swelling and a line of stitches that ran directly above my right eye. Even my perfect makeup couldn't fix this one.

A few days later, against the physicians' better judgment, I was released from the Picton hospital. Positive that going home was all I needed, I began a new chapter in my life. As my face scabbed over and the bruising yellowed, unexpected and relentless dizzy spells began to plague me. John was back to work, so my poor little girl did her best to alleviate my burden. As for Ben? Simply put, autism doesn't go away just because it's inconvenient. Parents and caregivers would agree that our jobs are 24/7.

Brain X-rays were ordered. To make a long story short, you know it's not your day when you hear the technician loudly request, "Get Mrs. Dunham's physician on the phone immediately!"

Less than twenty-four hours later, I was undergoing a full CAT scan. Though claustrophobic, I was too tired to care about that. Across the intercom, a faceless voice instructed me to stay very still. That was no problem for me, since in a strange way I was actually enjoying the peace and quiet.

I returned home after completing my morning with a visit to a neurosurgeon.

The test results detected blood pooled between my skull and my brain. But God was good and the blood dried up naturally. With the passage of time, the dizzy spells ebbed and I received a clean bill of health.

Afforded undeserved favour, I was given grace in the unexplained.

REFLECTION

Why did I recover from a brain injury when others do not? Why are some children born healthy and others suffer? Why do bad things happen to good people? Why is my son severely autistic, and profoundly learning disabled? What about all the injustice in the world?

Being perfectly honest, there are days when we just don't get it. Life doesn't always go according to our master plan, and we may never understand the reason things happen the way they do. Does that mean God isn't good? Does it mean He doesn't care? Absolutely not! God is good. He does care. But we are living in a fallen world. Our fight is not against flesh and blood but with the enemy of our souls.

Satan, knowing his time is short, does everything in his power to see humanity separated from God. Perhaps your own life is spinning out of control as you read this book. Like the cat on the limb, you're just "hanging in there, baby."

Take heart. God is sovereign. Despite our rebellion, sin, and wrong choices, He chose His perfect Son to be the way, the truth, and the life. The Creator of the universe willingly hung on a wooden cross. Never once did He call out, "Hey, this isn't fair! I'm not the guilty one here!" No. Rather He suffered all for a sinner such as me. *"It is finished"* (John 19:30), he cried out when the price was paid. Death and sin were conquered by the risen Saviour.

In James 4:14, we read that our time on earth is like vapour. During our few short years, we are offered the chance to receive or reject grace. Heaven awaits us. No, we may never understand why things happen the way they do, but then again, why would the Son of God willingly suffer for a wretch such as me?

Grace is the answer—unmerited favour, unlimited love, and unmitigated forgiveness.

He giveth more grace as our burdens grow greater,
    He sendeth more strength as our labors increase;
    To added afflictions He addeth His mercy,
    To multiplied trials He multiplies peace.

When we have exhausted our store of endurance,
    When our strength has failed ere the day is half
done,
    When we reach the end of our hoarded resources
    Our Father's full giving is only begun.

Fear not that thy need shall exceed His provision,
    Our God ever yearns His resources to share;
    Lean hard on the arm everlasting, availing;
    The Father both thee and thy load will upbear.

His love has no limits, His grace has no measure,
    His power no boundary known unto men;
    For out of His infinite riches in Jesus
    He giveth, and giveth, and giveth again.[13]

---

[13] Annie Johnson Flint, "He Giveth More Grace," 1941.

For we wrestle not against flesh and blood,
but against principalities, against powers,
against the rulers of the darkness of this
world, against spiritual wickedness in high
places. Wherefore take unto you the whole
armour of God, that ye may be able to
withstand in the evil day, and
having done all, to stand.
(Ephesians 6:12–13)

For my thoughts are not your thoughts,
neither are your ways my ways,
saith the Lord.
(Isaiah 55:8)

For what is your life? It is even a vapour,
that appeareth for a little time,
and then vanisheth away.
(James 4:14)

And he said unto me, My grace is sufficient
for thee: for my strength is made perfect in
weakness. Most gladly therefore will I rather
glory in my infirmities, that the power of
Christ may rest upon me.
(2 Corinthians 12:9)

But the God of all grace, who hath called
us unto his eternal glory by Christ Jesus,
after that ye have suffered a while, make you
perfect, stablish, strengthen, settle you.
(1 Peter 5:10)

And he said unto me, My grace is sufficient
for thee: for my strength is made perfect in
weakness. Most gladly therefore will I rather
glory in my infirmities, that the power of
Christ may rest upon me.
(2 Corinthians 12:9)

The Sunday School Lesson

Room dividers, visual aids, memory work, and cute little offering plates all spell one thing: Sunday school, 1970s style. When I consider the logistics it took to run a full departmental Sunday school, it absolutely boggles my mind. Back in the day, there was a teacher for each and every age. Evangelical churches boasted a class for everyone from the nursery right on through adults. Superintendents were responsible for ensuring curriculum was purchased, teachers trained, and attendance goals reached. And grand Christmas plays were performed annually.

Just thinking about it makes me feel tired.

What a time in history it was to be alive! Emerging from the sixties, the culture of the day was falling short. Family units were being redefined as secularism permeated everything from mainstream entertainment to the education system. Ideals were questioned, morality considered subjective, and sadly the church wasn't left unscathed. The televangelist movement was in full swing too. And although many TV ministries were bonafide, comedians delighted in lumping all Christians into one heap of religious fodder.

Though the issues were real, God was still on His throne, and He still had His people. Dedicated followers of Jesus recognized that it was time to take a stand. So what was the church to do? How do you reach a generation that increasingly believed the Bible was nothing more than a storybook?

A shift happened and a new tool was released into the Protestant community. The era of the mega bus ministry was born. Fleets of old buses began to fill church parking lots. Bus drivers, captains, and assistants flew into action. Events like Hamburger Sunday, Silver Dollar Sunday, Kite Sunday, and even Transistor Radio Sunday had kids ready to claim their rides to the house of the Lord. Each weekend, neighbourhoods saw at least two different church buses cross paths en route to Sunday school. Contests for attendance were loud, competitive, boisterous, and fun.

The bus ministry was blessed. Although its season is now past, it remains a vital chapter in church history. Even today you'll hear testimonies that begin with stories of kind bus workers who knocked on the doors of precious souls to invite them to church. The era was exciting and the promotions fun, but the winning of souls was priceless.

In 1975, my Sunday school experience didn't include a hip and happening class. In reality, my teacher was a kindly middle-aged woman with greying hair and a quiet spirit. Having raised a son who served as a missionary to Ecuador, this sweet woman became a hero to me. Dear, dear Mrs. Adams! I can't say her lessons came with any bells and whistles, but never once did I doubt her love or prayers for each girl who sat in her class.

On a very snowy December morning, I arrived at Sunday school and claimed my place next to Mrs. Adams. The weather that day led to sparse attendance, but no class was smaller than my grade's. I was the only one in my row. My mother taught the eleven-year-old girls across the aisle, so I was pretty sure I would be shuffled into her group when no one else showed up.

Following opening announcements, I was shocked when Mrs. Adams kindly directed me over to our regular meeting area. There we sat, one teacher and one awkward little girl. At first it felt strange, yet in no time at all I basked in the glory of being the star pupil. With no competition, I gladly answered every question.

Not only did I feel heard, I took it as my Christian duty to blurt out my latest sin. That past week, I had concocted a ridiculous scheme to smuggle one of my friends' puppies into our home. As preposterous and unrealistic as my idea was, my deception overwhelmed me with guilt. Mrs. Adams could have chuckled at my silly rambling, but rather she listened—and then thoughtfully unpacked a conversation about forgiveness, choices, honouring parents, and even temptation. That lesson remains vivid in my mind to this very day.

In her senior years, Mrs. Adams married Reverend Cecil Nelson. What precious friends the Nelsons were to my husband and myself. Decades have now passed since dear Mrs. Nelson graduated to heaven, but I will never forget that morning when she made me feel like I was the most important student in the world.

REFLECTION

I cheer for innovative programs and methods of spreading the Word of God. In fact, for many years I was a gospel ventriloquist; my husband was a Bible chalk talk artist. Big-picture ideas thrill me. It's imperative for supporting ministries to reach into communities.

Spread the good news! But never look past that one person who just shows up, or that quiet kid who blends into the woodwork. Your impact on an individual life runs deep. World evangelists are praiseworthy, but so are the gentle souls who furrow the ground, water the seeds, and patiently teach us the Word of God.

Jesus loves me, this I know,
    for the Bible tells me so.
    Little ones to him belong;
    they are weak, but he is strong.

Yes, Jesus loves me! Yes, Jesus loves me!
Yes, Jesus loves me! The Bible tells me so.[14]

And let us not be weary in well doing: for in due season we shall reap, if we faint not. (Galatians 6:9)

Let the word of Christ dwell in you richly in all wisdom; teaching and admonishing one another in psalms and hymns and spiritual songs, singing with grace in your hearts to the Lord. (Colossians 3:16)

---

[14] Anna Bartlett Warner, "Jesus Loves Me," 1859.

And daily in the temple, and in every house,
they ceased not to teach and
preach Jesus Christ.
(Acts 5:42)

THE RECIPE

Christmas 2023, my sister Mary Lu and I each received a very unique gift. Our sister Rhonda had acquired a photocopy of our grandmother's secret cookie recipe. This treasured find was particularly special since the directions were literally penned in our dear grandmother's handwriting. Having photocopied the precious script onto yellow cardstock, Rhonda had masterfully framed and wrapped these long-forgotten pieces of family history.

I immediately knew this was something I would always cherish. With a sense of destination, I began to scan grocery stores for the ingredients required to replicate these delicious treats. My journey had begun.

My grandmother lived with our family for my entire childhood. Her room was located across the hall from my room and her door was always open. There was never a time when we girls couldn't just walk in, flop across her neatly made bed, and just chat or watch a bit of television. At night, if I laid very still, I could hear her praying. It was comforting to fall asleep under her worship and quiet time with the Lord.

When I was thirteen, she graduated to heaven. Her death didn't come as a shock, since her body was worn and tired. During those latter days, she seemed restless. She longed to see her Saviour and was ready to go home.

Knowing her salvation was secure in Jesus, her life on the earth came to a quiet end. She left behind a godly heritage, having raised seven children who indeed were some of the finest

Christians I ever knew. Even now her future generations can rest knowing that they were loved and prayed for long before they were ever born.

So there I was in my kitchen, forty-six years after her death, measuring and combining the long-forgotten ingredients of her cookie recipe. With every dash of spice, childhood memories resurfaced.

Stalwart Grandmother Brown was in effect a part of the recipe of my life. Creaming together the butter and sugar, I pondered how much I was like her. This was the person who had influenced my love of vocabulary, writing, and memorizing both scripture and poetry. Listening to her quote literature or write out her thoughts in prose had ignited a passion in me to do the same. A no-nonsense Baptist, she hadn't spoiled or pampered her grandchildren. She'd taught us to honour the Lord's day and respect God's Word. While still enjoying laughter and the warmth of family, it had been her heart's desire to build godly character in each one of us. I aimed to please her—and as long as I returned her red pen and didn't talk during *The Price Is Right*, I pretty much remained in her good books.

Dropping cookie dough onto the large greased pans, I mused on the occasions we had eaten my grandmother's cookies. Never one to overdo or be wasteful, she had considered one cookie per person to be sufficient. Although secretly wishing for chocolate chips, I now realize that she would have deemed the walnuts and raisins to be healthy, and chocolate chips to be frivolous.

Continuing on my baking journey, I questioned my technique of combining the wet and dry ingredients. Some of the instructions were vague and I was grateful that Mary Lu had given me a few tips from her own kick at the can a few days prior. Were the spices sprinkled in evenly? Should I turn the oven down? After all, four hundred degrees seemed pretty high.

Second-guessing my every move, I grew aware of how sincerely I wanted to honour this project.

As I slid the first cookie sheet into the oven, a tiny pang pressed against my heart, for I had indeed tossed in "just a few" frivolous chocolate chips.

At last, the moment had come. With generational pride, I threw on my oven mitts and pulled out my much-anticipated creation. Drumroll please…

Each batch of cookies was nothing short of a triumph! I was in shock. They were perfect. With the aroma of nutmeg and cloves enveloping the room, I proudly displayed the cookies on a plate, right beside the framed instructions. Biting gingerly into the first cookie, I felt thankful. Yes, I was pleased with my baking—but more importantly, I felt grateful for the woman who had written the recipe.

REFLECTION

We should all hold dear the charge to influence and model godly character. When I'm gone, when you're gone, how will we be remembered? The ingredients we stir into the lives of those around us are priceless gifts. May the recipe of our lives be seasoned with grace, blessings, and always a dash of love.

The following poem, "Thanksgiving," was written by my grandmother, Fanny Brown:

Anything to be thankful for?
    And did I hear you complain?
    You are really downhearted and gloomy;
    Is it just because of the rain?
    Surely that is no reason dear,
    Get your thoughts on a higher plane,
    Think of your blessings and count them o'er
    And forget all about the rain.

God gives you food, clothing and health,
And manifold blessings each day.
So sing of God's love, and humbly kneel
In Thanksgiving, this Thanksgiving Day.

Praise ye the Lord. Blessed is the man that
feareth the Lord, that delighteth greatly
in his commandments. His seed shall be
mighty upon earth: the generation of the
upright shall be blessed. Wealth and riches
shall be in his house: and his righteousness
endureth for ever.
(Psalms 112:1–3)

And these words, which I command
thee this day, shall be in thine heart: and
thou shalt teach them diligently unto thy
children, and shalt talk of them when
thou sittest in thine house, and when thou
walkest by the way, and when thou liest
down, and when thou risest up. And thou
shalt bind them for a sign upon thine hand,
and they shall be as frontlets between thine
eyes. And thou shalt write them upon
the posts of thy house, and on thy gates.
(Deuteronomy 6:6–9)

THE FROSTED GLASS

In her lovely Spanish accent, my friend Alma assured me that she was praying for the Lord to bless my writing.

Alma, along with the other wonderful ladies of our Wednesday morning Bible study, inspire and encourage my soul. Prayer support from such godly women has truly been a gift of matchless worth. Even when we don't know exactly what's happening in each other's lives, we pray one for another… and God answers prayer. Being vulnerable to share my story requires patience and humility, but most of all it requires prayer.

Once again, let me unpack another episode of my strange but definitely prayed-over life. Welcome to the scene of my living room…

Approaching midnight, Ben was wide awake finishing up a bowl of hamburger and pasta. My husband was sound asleep upstairs and my daughter and I had just completed our nightly puzzle competition—yes, that is a thing in our house.

Despite it being mid-February, Christmas music wafted in the background. It would have all been so idyllic except for one teensy tiny detail: Ben was spiralling into a horrible meltdown. As he stomped on the floor and hollered for his father to wake up, I knew this was just the beginning. Ugh!

When it seemed things couldn't get more miserable, he took a flying leap into our front hallway—an action which was followed by a loud *crash*. Within a split second, the picture window of our sunroom door was broken into a million pieces.

Oh great! Not another window!

The house was old, and the old glass didn't just crack. It shattered.

I frantically pulled Ben from the carnage to check his wrists for blood. Buffered by the venetian blind, my son was spared from so much as a scratch. Grateful for God's protection, my carnal eyes shifted to the mess. Clad in pyjamas and slippers, I reconciled myself to gathering up all the shards. Tired and not feeling overly spiritual, I was one grouchy mama.

I scotch-taped cardstock over the large hole in the door. Although not pretty, at least the cold would be prevented from entering our little hallway.

The process took well over an hour—and by the time it was completed, I was exhausted.

And as for Ben? Well, he was now ordering cheese—literally. What a night!

Contemplating the current situation, I needed a game plan. That's when I had a lightbulb moment. Plexiglass! Yes, I would go online and order a sheet of unbreakable plexiglass—really, really thick plexiglass! After all, if it was good enough for my beloved Maple Leafs, it was good enough for me too.

Scrolling the internet revealed that plexiglass isn't cheap. Finances aside, with the click of a button my order was placed. I was soon to be the proud owner of a hunk of overpriced plastic!

A few days later, a massive flat box was deposited on my front steps. With lofty anticipation, I tore the package open. Much like Scarlett O'Hara's "I'll never be hungry again" speech, my inward monologue consisted of "This window will never, ever break again!"

Sliding back the protective cardboard, my heart dropped. The plexiglass was frosted! It would be virtually impossible to view anything through the obscured blur. Bemoaning the fact that I would never again have the luxury of looking out that window, I laid the opaque panel against the wall. I willfully shifted my thoughts and chose to focus on one thing: John would be repairing the door on Monday morning.

The following night, I discussed the pros and cons of the frosted look with my daughter. Obviously weary of my ridiculous obsession, Katie brightly mentioned how nice it was that the window had arrived scratch-free. I admired her positive point of view and reconsidered.

Squealing in delight, we suddenly questioned whether the windowpane was actually frosted at all. Was the frost real or was it only a protective covering?

Gingerly scraping our fingernails across the corner of the plexiglass revealed a new reality. As the filmy white covering peeled away, we at last saw the true product.

I called my husband to come quickly. The three of us then marvelled and laughed, for the crazy pane was beautifully transparent. Okay, I need to say it: it was as clear as glass!

REFLECTION

We read in 1 Corinthians 13:12, *"For now we see through a glass, darkly; but then face to face: now I know in part; but then shall I know even as I am known."*

When the plexiglass first arrived, I was so focused on the frosted covering that the truth was obscured from my eyes. Yet once the film was ripped away, my vision was unfettered. I then saw the bigger picture… it all made sense.

We inhabit a gauzy and clouded world. As humans, our finite minds are limited. Our outlook is murky and uninspired. Trials veiled in tears make it difficult to see God's hand in our lives.

The apostle Paul teaches in 1 Corinthians that we actually view life through a clouded glass. No wonder scripture admonishes us to live by faith and not by sight. Life on the earth is only a precursor to eternity. Be inspired that one day the veil will be lifted, the mist will peel away, and we will be home. No more frosted glass!

> Sing the wondrous love of Jesus,
>   Sing His mercy and His grace;
>   In the mansions bright and blessed
>   He'll prepare for us a place.
>
> When we all get to heaven,
>   what a day of rejoicing that will be!
>   When we all see Jesus,
>   we'll sing and shout the victory!
>
> While we walk the pilgrim pathway
>   Clouds will overspread the sky;
>   But when trav'ling days are over
>   Not a shadow, not a sigh.
>
> Let us then be true and faithful,
>   Trusting, serving ev'ry day;
>   Just one glimpse of Him in glory
>   Will the toils of life repay.
>
> Onward to the prize before us!
>   Soon His beauty we'll behold;
>   Soon the pearly gates will open—
>   We shall tread the streets of gold.[15]

---

[15] E.E. Hewitt, "When We All Get to Heaven," 1898.

For now we see through a glass, darkly; but
then face to face: now I know in part; but
then shall I know even as also I am known.
(1 Corinthians 13:12)

But we all, with open face beholding as in a
glass the glory of the Lord, are changed into
the same image from glory to glory,
even as by the Spirit of the Lord.
(2 Corinthians 3:18)

When a Compliment Doesn't Sound Like a Compliment

Age may bring wisdom, but unfortunately it throws in a few little extra gifts as well: crepey skin, grey roots, laugh lines, and, dare I say it, the odd chin hair. Yikes! Being the baby in my family, somehow I never pictured these atrocities happening to me. But time marched on and now I'm indeed the woman in the grocery aisle who extols to young moms, "Enjoy your little ones. They grow up so quickly."

Never one for sports, there are no dusty athletic awards in my attic to remind me of a time when I could run fast or hit a home run. On the other hand, old photos undeniably reveal the truth: I am no longer a spring chicken. I've lived through the era of bad perms, blue eyeshadow, and even the dreaded mullet.

Yet still I have no idea where time went.

I've been married now for four decades and my husband has been my cheerleader, prayer partner, confidant, and thankfully that one special person who can always make me laugh. Through thick and thin, he has consistently led our family with faith, grace, and humour.

At the same time, there was one certain day when my better half wasn't exactly in my good books.

It was a sticky summer afternoon. Between running after Ben, humidity melting my makeup, and my hair resembling something the cat had dragged in, I wasn't exactly a candidate for Miss Congeniality. The mirror wasn't my friend and quite frankly I felt old.

This is where John enters the story. Poor sweet, innocent, unsuspecting John. He had no idea how my next question was going to land him in some pretty hot water.

"When we were first dating, what did you find attractive about me?" I snapped out, seeking an ego boost.

Looking like a deer caught in headlights, John processed my challenge. He paused and thought about it. That may have been fine… until he thought some more.

The quietness was deafening.

His answer surely wasn't coming quick enough. How hard could this possibly be? At one point, I vainly hoped he was having trouble narrowing down his options. Was he recalling my long blonde hair? My eyes would be an answer. Or possibly my smile. Maybe he was going to play it safe and just say that I was pretty.

Truth be told, at this stage I was practically ready to accept the fact that I had decent posture!

Following what felt like an eternity—or at the very least, forty seconds—my dear, naive husband broke the silence by blurting out possibly the worst answer in the entire world.

"You were very clean."

Dumbfounded, I stared at him blankly. Was he kidding me? Clean? Surely this was his attempt at a joke. The best he could come up with… was that I had decent hygiene?

The bar must have been set pretty low back then. Apparently, he had based his attraction to me based on my use of soap and water.

If he decided to follow this up with a commentary about my nice personality, I would go bananas. But since going bananas wasn't really my thing, I did him one worse.

I enacted the dreaded *silent treatment*.

Poor John, God bless him, stood tripping over his words and desperately trying to make things right. Blurting out anything that came to mind, he dug himself into an even deeper hole.

The silent treatment naturally morphed to the next level: the *steel eyeball.*

Apologizing profusely, my dear husband did the only other thing he could think of: he made me laugh.

So much for the silent treatment.

I don't recall exactly what he said to crack me up, but it definitely had to do with him wanting me to write him a script. Dropping to the floor, we laughed until our stomachs hurt. Once again all seemed right with the world.

Tension gone, my sweet husband clarified what he had meant by calling me clean. In a lightbulb moment, I realized that his comment had been a word of kindness. Rather than silly flattery, John was appreciative of my life choices. This wasn't about having perfect makeup or the latest hairstyle; it was about how he valued me as a person.

At last I understood. Despite my pride and snarky attitude, John had gifted me the compliment of grace.

REFLECTION

One day we will all stand before God. Whether we baked cookies, went to church, or helped a little old lady cross the street, it won't cover our sin. Good deeds are wonderful, but they don't equal a clean heart.

Romans 23:3 makes it very clear that we have all sinned and fall short of God's glory.

Putting it plainly: on our own, we are a mess. Painting good over the bad only leaves us smeared and wanting. Ugly baggage has no place in heaven.

But God, in His grace, sent us the rescue plan. His perfect Son Jesus came to bear our sin on the cross, defeat death, and rise again.

Read John 3:16. That says it all. God really does love you. Eternal life is offered as a gift of grace through faith. Only Jesus can forgive the repentant heart… only He can make us clean.

Search me, O God, and know my heart today;
    Try me, O Savior, know my thoughts, I pray.
    See if there be some wicked way in me;
    Cleanse me from ev'ry sin and set me free.

I praise thee, Lord, for cleansing me from sin;
    Fulfill thy Word, and make me pure within.
    Fill me with fire where once I burned with shame;
    Grant my desire to magnify thy name.[16]

---

[16] J. Edwin Orr, "Search Me, O God," 1913.

That if thou shalt confess with thy mouth
the Lord Jesus, and shalt believe in thine
heart that God hath raised him from the
dead, thou shalt be saved. For with the heart
man believeth unto righteousness; and with
the mouth confession is made
unto salvation.
(Romans 10:9–10)

For by grace are ye saved through faith; and
that not of yourselves: it is the gift of God:
not of works, lest any man should boast.
(Ephesians 2:8–9)

THE LONG NIGHT

Having just completed the morning announcements at church, I said "God bless you this morning" and returned to my seat in the second row. My husband reached over and gave my hand a reassuring squeeze. As the worship team transitioned into their next song, I breathed out a prayer of thanks. Knowing that my parents had been cheering me on via YouTube warmed my heart.

Church is my happy place. Greeting and encouraging my Bridge Whitby family gives me joy. And as the congregation looked on, I couldn't help but think of how no one there would ever have guessed the long night I had just endured.

With Ben's sleeping issues, bedtime usually occurs between one and two in the morning. Strangely, and thankfully, I am pretty cool about that. I'm definitely tougher than I was in my younger days and commonly burn the midnight oil.

Yet my lack of rest went to a whole new level that particular weekend.

It had been a typical Saturday. As evening approached, I was delighted that the next day it would be my turn to attend church. Gluing on my false fingernails, I mentally prepared for the announcements I would deliver during the morning service.

Reminding Ben to be good for the girls, John bade us each goodnight. Like a fine-oiled machine, our family began the night shift…

Swaying back and forth in his rocking chair, Ben awaited Katie to cue his music. The routine was the same old, same old. Standing by the stove, I had already commenced preparing Ben's nightly pasta. Step by step, line by line, each of us was doing our part to have a peace-filled night.

Despite every valiant effort, another manic episode was about to crash over us.

Ben pounded both feet on the floor and hollered at the top of his lungs, his eyes glazed over with confusion. Jumping out of my skin, I rushed to the living room. I firmly reassured my son that everything was okay and employed every tactic in the book. I sought to distract and redirect his attention. Then I sang and read to him from his favourite books.

I longed for a normal life and prayed desperately.

Sadly, my every effort to defuse the situation was met with screaming, kicking, and scratching. Kate and I looked helplessly at each other. Even the medication prescribed for times like these had very little effect.

The noise was deafening. I dreaded that someone walking by our home might hear the reverberation and phone the police.

Seeking to intervene, John came downstairs numerous times. His presence only exacerbated our son's aggressive behaviour. Ben plugged his ears, unable to endure the decibels of his own voice.

At my wit's end, I worried that John was going to have a heart attack. I raised my own voice over the din and sent my husband back to bed. Sleep was not the objective; I knew he would pray… and at this point prayer was our only hope.

By three o'clock in the morning, the situation had improved only slightly. As I sang another stanza of "Love Lifted Me," Katie quietly retreated to her room. I sang hoarsely as Ben yelled intermittently and stomped his feet. Hymn after hymn, song after song, I pondered my son's mental anguish with bleary eyes and a broken heart. I clung to every verse, knowing that Jesus loved my family.

At four-thirty, exhausted and unable to carry on any further, Ben trudged up the stairs and dropped onto his bed. With that, my thirty-year-old son, emotionally drained, fell asleep.

Numbly I walked to my room. How would I possibly get up for church the next morning?

Cruelly, the enemy swung into action. "How do you expect to welcome anyone anywhere tomorrow?" he demanded. "You, doing the announcements? That's a good laugh. It's unfair how you and Katie have to take turns caring for Ben on Sunday mornings. After all, you only want to go to church. You are old. Who do you think you are anyway? You're a mess. You're a failure. No one understands what your family endures. Give up, give up, give up…"

As this attack unfolded, all I could choke out was a simple prayer: "Thank You, Lord, for this pillow. And thank You for this blanket."

Immediately I fell into a deep sleep.

Two and a half hours later, my alarm rang. Gulping down a cup of coffee, I threw on perhaps a little too much makeup. John and I grabbed our Bibles and dashed out the door.

Strangely, I experienced a sweet sense of joy that morning as I welcomed people and delivered the announcements. This wasn't a silly, giggly emotion but rather a deep-seated, God-given peace. We had made it through one more long night… and the icing on the cake was that I felt completely rested.

REFLECTION

What is your long night? Whether dreading the future or reliving the past, the hours on the clock can tick by relentlessly. Perhaps you're agonizing over a child who's making poor choices. Did the doctor speak devastating words you never dreamed of hearing? Is your caregiving journey more than you expected?

Whether you're broken-hearted or facing monumental loss, God sees it all.

Not one of us is immune to long and weary nights. When I was young, Mom would tell me that everything would look better in the morning… and sometimes it does. Other times it doesn't.

When all you can do is choke out "Thank You, Lord, for this pillow, and thank You for this blanket," close your eyes. Only Jesus can give rest to the soul. As the old hymn says, "When nothing else could help, love lifted me…"

> I was sinking deep in sin,
>> Far from the peaceful shore,
>> Very deeply stained within,
>> Sinking to rise no more;
>> But the Master of the sea
>> Heard my despairing cry,
>> From the waters lifted me–
>> Now safe am I.

> Love lifted me,
>> Love lifted me,
>> When nothing else could help,
>> Love lifted me;
>> Love lifted me,
>> Love lifted me,
>> When nothing else could help,
>> Love lifted me.[17]

---

[17] James Rowe, "Love Lifted Me," 1912.

Come unto me, all ye that labour and
are heavy laden, and I will give you rest.
(Matthew 11:28)

Now the God of hope fill you with all joy
and peace in believing, that ye may abound
in hope, through the power
of the Holy Ghost.
(Romans 15:13)

THE LEGACY OF FRIENDSHIP

During the mid-1980s, my Aunt Ruby relayed a humorous story to my mother. She, her husband Ken, and their son Bill had invited over the new associate pastor for a meal. Pastor Rob arrived with his very pregnant wife, Dot, and their little girl, Jill. The family was delightful and my Aunt Ruby's gift of hospitality that evening took on the form of a lovely roast beef dinner.

Yet it was missed by no one that the bubbly pastor's wife was steadily growing quiet. For indeed Dot was in labour.

Completing her roast beef dinner, she firmly stated, "I will not leave until I eat my slice of apple pie."

With dessert accomplished, and little Jill handed over to my aunt and uncle, Pastor Rob could finally rush his dear wife to the hospital.

A little over an hour later, a precious baby boy was ushered into the world. His name was Jordan.

Skipping forward ten years, our church in Whitby was welcoming the very same family to join our pastoral family. What an honour it was to forge a friendship with the very people my aunt had told us about so many years ago.

And thus it was that we watched both Jill and Jordan grow into vibrant happy teenagers.

During this chapter in our lives, Ben's behaviour was making church attendance difficult for our family. Bombarded by trial medications and what felt like one too many diagnoses, Ben's tolerance for crowds and noise was reaching a breaking point. Sunday after Sunday, my family nervously camouflaged ourselves against the back wall of the auditorium. Primed to exit stage left at any given moment, we braced ourselves for anything from a bloodcurdling scream to a bite. Ben was like a ticking timebomb—and heaven help us all if he even thought he heard a baby cry.

Discouraged and suffering from a clear case of sleep deprivation, my default response was to make any excuse in the book to stay home. I would hide my tears, and messy mascara, under the guise of being little Miss Perfect.

Yet God saw my exhaustion and understood my embarrassment… and He had a plan.

The same baby who had come mighty close to being born in my Aunt Ruby's dining room was now a young man—and he was hearing the call to stand in the gap. When the preaching began on Sunday mornings, Jordan would step away from his friends in their comfortable pew to help the mom of the little boy sitting against the back wall. Sauntering down the aisle, Jordan would look at Ben and say, "Come on, buddy." These were the only three words my son ever needed to hear. Anticipating a trip to the gym, Ben would make a beeline down the hall.

Never putting on a show, Jordan simply recognized a need and bravely heeded the call.

Well over two decades have now passed since that special chapter in my son's life. Jordan has moved on and is now happily married with children of his own. As for Ben, he remains the same—and to him, Jordan will forever be etched in his mind as the teenaged boy who called him Buddy.

REFLECTION

Where are you right now? What simple gift can you share to unburden someone's load? Kingdom business doesn't need to be complicated. A kind email, word of encouragement, or perhaps meal to help out a frazzled mom could be the very thing that touches a person's heart for eternity. And maybe, just maybe, you'll be blessed enough to be forever remembered as someone's buddy.

Give of your best to the Master;
Give of the strength of your youth;
Throw your soul's fresh, glowing ardor
Into the battle for truth.
Jesus has set the example,
Dauntless was He, young and brave;
Give Him your loyal devotion;
Give Him the best that you have.

Give of your best to the Master;
Give of the strength of your youth;
Clad in salvation's full armor,
Join in the battle for truth.

Give of your best to the Master;
Give Him first place in your heart;
Give Him first place in your service;
Consecrate every part.
Give, and to you will be given;
God His beloved Son gave;
Gratefully seeking to serve Him,
Give Him the best that you have.

Give of your best to the Master;
    Naught else is worthy His love;
    He gave Himself for your ransom,
    Gave up His glory above.
    Laid down His life without murmur,
    You from sin's ruin to save;
    Give Him your heart's adoration,
    Give Him the best that you have.[18]

---

[18] Howard B. Grose, "Give of Your Best to the Master," 1900.

He hath shewed thee, O man, what is good;
and what doth the Lord require of thee, but
to do justly, and to love mercy, and to walk
humbly with thy God?
(Micah 6:8)

Put on therefore, as the elect of God,
holy and beloved, bowels of mercies,
kindness, humbleness of mind,
meekness, longsuffering…
(Colossians 3:12)

For I was an hungred, and ye gave me meat:
I was thirsty, and ye gave me drink: I was a
stranger, and ye took me in: naked, and ye
clothed me: I was sick, and ye visited me: I
was in prison, and ye came unto me. Then
shall the righteous answer him, saying, Lord,
when saw we thee an hungred, and fed thee?
or thirsty, and gave thee drink? When saw we
thee a stranger, and took thee in? or naked,
and clothed thee? Or when saw we thee sick,
or in prison, and came unto thee? And the
King shall answer and say unto them, Verily
I say unto you, Inasmuch as ye have done it
unto one of the least of these my brethren, ye
have done it unto me.
(Matthew 25:35–40)

Grace to Do the Next Thing

Stuffing down feelings of inadequacy, I took my place at our ladies' morning Bible study. Life was complicated and I felt "stuck." With the enemy clumping all my problems into one gigantic blob, my experience was that of frustration and exhaustion.

Providentially, as our pastor's wife, Kathy taught the lesson. She was saying exactly what I needed to hear. Citing the life of the famous missionary Elisabeth Elliot, Kathy encouraged our group with the following words: "Just do the next thing." At face value, those words may sound trite, but the story behind them is both powerful and life-challenging.

Elisabeth and Jim Elliot were a young married couple serving as missionaries in the Ecuadorian jungle. With the birth of their daughter Valarie in 1955, it seemed there was nothing this powerhouse couple couldn't do.

Yet tragedy hit when Jim and four other male missionaries were speared to death by the very tribe with whom they had come to share the gospel. Thus, on January 8, 1956, Elisabeth became a young widowed mother.

As newspapers reported the death of the five young missionaries, Elisabeth prayed for strength.

Bravely returning to Ecuador, Elisabeth continued her mission. She chose to raise her little girl among the very people who had murdered her husband, thus continuing her life's calling. With love and patience, the gospel was proclaimed and countless souls, including the men who had murdered Jim, found forgiveness and salvation.

In later years when Elisabeth was questioned about how she handled so many losses in her life, she would often quote a line from an old English poem. The line was this: "do the next thing."

As Kathy shared Elizabeth's quote, my attitude awakened. "Do the next thing." Wow! I had never broken down my challenges into such practical terms. From calming meltdowns to cleaning up broken glass, I too am required *to do the next thing.*

This stanza appears in the poem "Do the Next Thing":

Do it immediately, do it with prayer;
Do it reliantly, casting all care;
Do it with reverence, tracing His hand
Who placed it before thee with earnest command.
Stayed on Omnipotence, safe 'neath His wing,
Leave all results, do the next thing.[19]

REFLECTION

In the mid-1980s, I was privileged to attend a conference where Elisabeth Elliot was the guest speaker. Having read her book, *Through the Gates of Splendor,*[20] I was excited to meet this hero of the faith. Older and retired, it was difficult to picture this gracious woman living in the Ecuadorian rainforest.

Having purchased her latest book, I was honoured to have her autograph it for me.

---

[19] Eleanor Amerman Sutphen, *Ye Nexte Thynge* (New York, NY: Fleming H. Revell, 1897).
[20] Elisabeth Elliot, *Through Gates of Splendor* (New York, NY: Harper & Brothers, 1957).

I yearn to be faithful on my own journey and realize how weak I really am. I complain, compare, and often feel sorry for myself. My life falls short.

Yet one day this life will make sense when I see my Saviour. Yes, Jesus, who saved me by His grace, is the author of my story. My son will know peace and his mind will be clear. But until that day, I must be faithful to "do the next thing."

But until that day, through chapters of autism I will find stories of grace.

Thou wilt shew me the path of life: in thy
presence is fulness of joy; at thy right hand
there are pleasures for evermore.
(Psalms 16:11)

Looking unto Jesus the author and finisher
of our faith; who for the joy that was set
before him endured the cross, despising the
shame, and is set down at the right hand of
the throne of God.
(Hebrews 12:2)

He brought me up also out of an horrible
pit, out of the miry clay, and set my feet
upon a rock, and established my goings.
(Psalms 40:2)

THE BEJEWELLED BOX

Gently lifting the tiny cardboard lid, my eyes widened. Unbidden tears flowed as mascara smeared my face…

Hmmm. Perhaps it's best if I back up.

In 2020, when COVID-19 reared its ugly head, news bulletins gripped our hearts at the declaration of a global pandemic. Within only a few short months, my husband had the heart-wrenching task of presiding over the funeral of a dear friend whose life was cut short by this terrible virus. Social distancing, online church services, masking, toilet paper shortages, and learning how to use video conferencing became our new normal.

During this timeframe, I also noticed that my son's front tooth was somewhat discoloured. With no dental offices open, I instructed my husband to do a more proficient job of brushing Ben's teeth. Poor John, who faithfully cared for all our son's hygienic needs, found himself once again in hot water.

Naively I told myself that this was only cosmetic. After all, all of Ben's teeth had been sealed. What could possibly go wrong?

Yet as the dental clinics remained locked, the tooth continued to darken.

Then it happened. The tooth broke… and I freaked out.

Providentially, it was at this time that the government cautiously once again allowed restricted access to dental care.

But we had another issue: Ben wouldn't wear a mask. All our attempts to use personal protective equipment were met with hysterics and shortness of breath. With no plan B in sight, I phoned the dentist and pleaded for help. With compassion and dignity, the clinic set out a timeframe for us to usher Ben into the clinic for a private appointment.

Examining each and every tooth, the staff treated our son as though he was the only patient in the world. With the bribery—oops, I mean promise—of Chinese food, Ben behaved quite well.

I prayed for an easy fix and allowed myself to take a deep breath… but that breath didn't last very long. Ben's front tooth was the least of his dental issues. The X-rays revealed extensive and quite serious underlying complications.

Ben was going to need an orthodontic surgeon.

Willing myself to inhale, the narrative skipped from bad to worse. Due to our son being over the age of eighteen, as his biological parents we had absolutely no legal authority to authorize sedation or surgery.

It was like we were frozen in time. There we stood with an adult son, with the cognitive understanding of a three-year-old, being informed that we had to petition the court for legal guardianship.

Considering that my knowledge of the judicial system had come from watching *Judge Judy* and old black-and-white episodes of *Perry Mason*, I frantically scrolled for a lawyer.

Discovering a firm that oversaw cases such as ours, I paid the retainer fee. The first installment came to $3,600. This was going to be a very expensive year! Dusting off our credit card, we knew that God saw it all.

Then the real work began. I sifted through drawers, boxes, folders, and old envelopes, since I was required to show verification of every doctor's letter we had ever received, from specialists to psychologists. The speech and language reports, audiology testing, and certification of disability were to be archived in numerical order.

Triumphing over each document found was a bittersweet experience. I sadly recalled the birth of my precious baby boy, back when I'd had no idea that one day I would be working to have him declared incompetent.

Staring down at my dining room table, covered with legal paperwork, I felt overwhelmed. All these meticulous projections, budgets, daily routines, dietary needs, and even toileting issues had to be written out in agonizing detail. I had to describe Ben's personal effects alongside a thorough description of our home's layout. And by the time I chronicled my son's need for medications, including antipsychotics and antidepressants, I felt nothing short of raw.

It hurt to understand that we were to be treated no differently than anyone else seeking legal guardianship. I cried, feeling overwhelmed, and my husband prayed. Between sleep deprivation, unending paperwork, and Ben being just plain Ben, I self-medicated on pizza, coffee, and anything chocolate.

Following two months of organizing and practically writing an exhaustive biography of our son's life, John and I returned to the lawyer's office. I squeezed the mint green file folder in my hands and then reluctantly handed over all my work, which I considered to be a work of art by this point.

"Thank you," said the receptionist.

Indignation rose in my chest and my mind scrambled. "Thank you"? Was she kidding me? I'd poured my son's life onto these neatly labelled sheets! I had agonized, scrutinized, and even used colour-coded tabs! And all I got was a simple "Thank you"?

A wave of silent sadness crashed over me. My pride was bruised. Although I longed to be Super Mom, Spiritual Mom, or even Cool Mom, I was just plain Weary Mom. I did what I always did: I smiled my Christian smile, thanked the receptionist, straightened my shoulders, and walked out the door.

With the court system backed up, we were now in for a long wait. Days rolled into weeks and weeks rolled into months. Ben's front tooth deteriorated to one-third of its original size as the molar issues worsened. Only by divine intervention was my son spared pain or infection.

We phoned and emailed for updates only to be assured that we would be informed when a court date was secured. Without the precious prayers of friends and family, I wasn't sure I could take any more stress.

Practically nine months to the day after this journey began, our petition was heard. With the sweep of the judge's pen, we were granted full legal guardianship of our son. Joy, relief, and thankfulness enveloped our hearts. Armed with an official certificate, complete with a gold seal, we were finally ready to get the job done.

Thankful to have the procedure set for February 2023, we trusted God to keep us calm. Tensions rose, though, as we now faced more than $8,600 in lawyer and dental fees. The funny part is that the man of the hour, Ben, was oblivious to all that was happening. His comprehension level was such that he simply understood that we were going to see a "very special dentist"—and more importantly: "Good boys get Chinese food."

The morning prior to the operation, our Pastor, his sweet wife Kathy, and our dear friends Wayne and Sandy—yes, the same Sandy who was my amazing Kindergarten teacher—arrived at our home to pray. Hiding my frazzled heart, I threw on my makeup and spread the table with tea and goodies. I was on autopilot.

The fellowship was sweet and, quite frankly, a welcome distraction. Comforted by a time of prayer, we were once again reminded that God was in control.

Then the unexpected happened. Kathy and Sandy produced a cute little box bejewelled with tiny plastic diamonds. Clearing her throat, as only a seasoned teacher could do, Sandy began to speak.

"John and Lynn, your church family loves you very much," she said. "So much that I am not sure that you realize just how loved you truly are."

We smiled politely as Sandy continued.

"Without your knowledge, the small groups at the church have joined forces to create what we have deemed Project Benjamin. Please open this little box and accept this love gift from your church family."

Reaching across the table, Sandy placed the bejewelled box in my hand. I lifted the small cardboard lid and felt overwhelmed. Before my eyes lay enough money to cover all our lawyer fees and dental costs.

Unable to take it all in, I thought I was going to faint. In one providential sweep of God's mighty hand, our debts were paid.

Speechless, John and I broke into tears. So much for my mascara!

As I looked up into the smiling faces of these dear friends, I knew that we were on holy ground. Despite my worry, impatience, and ever-present need to fix things, I was lavished with his grace. I will cherish this moment forever.

Laughter broke out when Kathy chimed in, "There is even enough money to get Ben his Chinese food!"

The following day, after two hours of anaesthesia, the operation was deemed a success. Some teeth were saved while others were not, but the icing on the cake was that my son had a brand-new smile!

Swollen and wobbly from the effects of the sedation, it took four attendants and my husband to guide all two hundred thirty pounds of our six-foot-four son back to the car.

When the attending nurse questioned what Ben was mumbling, my husband smiled and replied, "Chinese rice."

All praise be to God! Project Benjamin was completed.

REFLECTION

My words are too weak to express my gratitude. I do believe that Thomas O Chrisholm said it far better than me when he penned the following words:

Great is thy faithfulness, O God, my Father;
There is no shadow of turning with thee.
Thou changest not, thy compassions, they fail not;
As thou hast been, thou forever wilt be.

Great is thy faithfulness,
Great is thy faithfulness,
Morning by morning new mercies I see.
All I have needed thy hand hast provided;
Great is thy faithfulness,
Lord unto me.[21]

---

[21] Thomas O Chisholm, "Great Is Thy Faithfulness," 1923.

He that dwelleth in the secret place of the
most High shall abide under the shadow of the
Almighty. I will say of the Lord, He is my refuge
and my fortress: my God; in him will I trust.
Surely he shall deliver thee from the snare of
the fowler, and from the noisome pestilence.
He shall cover thee with his feathers, and under
his wings shalt thou trust: his truth shall be thy
shield and buckler. Thou shalt not be afraid for
the terror by night; nor for the arrow that flieth
by day; nor for the pestilence that walketh in
darkness; nor for the destruction that wasteth
at noonday. A thousand shall fall at thy side,
and ten thousand at thy right hand; but it shall
not come nigh thee. Only with thine eyes shalt
thou behold and see the reward of the wicked.
Because thou hast made the Lord, which is my
refuge, even the most High, thy habitation;
there shall no evil befall thee, neither shall any
plague come nigh thy dwelling. For he shall
give his angels charge over thee, to keep thee
in all thy ways. They shall bear thee up in their
hands, lest thou dash thy foot against a stone.
Thou shalt tread upon the lion and adder: the
young lion and the dragon shalt thou trample
under feet. Because he hath set his love upon
me, therefore will I deliver him: I will set him
on high, because he hath known my name. He
shall call upon me, and I will answer him: I will
be with him in trouble; I will deliver him, and
honour him. With long life will I satisfy him,
and shew him my salvation.

(Psalms 91:1–16)

It is of the Lord's mercies that we are not
consumed, because his compassions fail
not. They are new every morning: great is
thy faithfulness. The Lord is my portion,
saith my soul; therefore will I hope in him.
(Lamentations 3:22–24)

But my God shall supply all your need
according to his riches in glory
by Christ Jesus.
(Philippians 4:19)

Faithfulness Behind and Ahead of Our Story

For a number of years, I have savoured opportunities to share my journey. One of the first times I shared my story was with a ladies group in Oshawa, Ontario. My son was only seven years old at the time, and during that chapter of autism my arms were covered in bruises, bites, and scratches.

As the evening drew to a close, I gathered my purse and Bible to go home. As I prepared to exit, a woman questioned me about whether I shared my testimony often. I admitted that this was a fresh endeavour.

She locked her eyes with mine. "I'm sure this is going to be the first of many more times for you," she stated firmly but kindly.

More than two decades later, I am indeed grateful for each and every opportunity I have been blessed with to tell my story.

I enjoy speaking. Encouraging others encourages me. In the wise words of C.S. Lewis,

---

"Friendship… is born the moment when one man
says to another, 'What! You too? I thought
that no one but myself…'"[22]

I fondly recall speaking with the women's group at my home church. It was a lovely fall day. With COVID-19 restrictions

[22] C.S. Lewis, *The Four Loves* (Toronto, ON: Harper Collins, 1960), 49.

slightly lifted, the ladies were just thankful to attend anything in person. God blessed our time together.

Then life continued on as usual. What I didn't realize was that the Lord was birthing an idea in the heart of Kathy, my pastor's wife.

Sitting at a luncheon a few weeks later, Kathy effortlessly swayed the conversation. "Lynn, I do believe there is a book in you."

Deflecting, I nervously babbled something about a fictional tale I had written and photocopied for some friends.

But going home that day, I couldn't shake Kathy's words. A book inside of me? Could that be actually true?

I acknowledged the many times I had searched for a devotional that broached the subject of autism. Was it possible that I could be a catalyst for people caught up in the unexpected?

The nudge to write a book was real, but regretfully so was my decision to ignore it.

Not long thereafter, while exchanging emails with my cousin Lois, she also suggested that I should write a book, even though she had no idea of my encounter with Kathy. Having great respect for my cousin, I felt humbled by her comment. I tucked her wisdom into my heart. The little nudge was growing more acute.

Months passed before another dear friend approached me.

"Lynn, I wanted a chance to talk with you," said Leslie, smiling. "I really think God wants you to write a book. It's so easy to listen to you speak. If you wrote a book, I would buy it!"

It would be an understatement to say that her words caught me off-guard. Was the Lord actually speaking to me through all these wise, godly women?

Now here's the kicker. Within days of my conversation with Leslie, I was watching *The 700 Club* on the television in my living room. The co-host, Terry Meeuwsen, was praying when my attention was brought to full alert. I heard her say, "God is speaking to someone about writing a book. You don't really want to write a book, but you should. There are people who need to hear what you have to say."

Believe me—for an old-school Baptist, a fundamental, hymn-singin', King-James-Bible-totin' kind of gal, things like this don't just happen every day!

The little nudge became my prayer, and my prayer became my mission. I was going to write a devotional. Stemming from personal experience, my passion was to encourage, bless, and offer biblical hope to those who found themselves in "the unexpected."

My husband prayed over me for God's guidance.

Then, only days later, John strutted in through the door with a gift. Pledging unconditional support, he blessed me with a brand-new laptop. Until that day, the only tech I'd ever owned was my cell phone and a refurbished tablet. It felt like Christmas!

Excited, speechless, and terrified, my adventure had begun.

I gathered with my Wednesday morning life group and shared my decision. Keen to the significance of this project, these special ladies kept me both accountable and focused. I will always cherish their intercessory prayers.

More than one year after I first laid my fingers across the keyboard of that new laptop, I am approaching the last leg of the journey. Will this project go anywhere? I have no idea. But this one thing I do know: God has been my guide each step of the way. Blanketed in prayer and encouragement, I have written, erased, rewritten, and edited the words more times than I care to remember.

My biggest obstacle has been giving myself permission to be vulnerable. At times I worried about whether I overshared. I didn't want to look inept at life.

Paradoxically, I have felt freedom—the freedom to recognize God's strength in my weakness and the freedom to quietly trust. In the school of the unexpected, in the chaos of broken windows, bumps, bites, and messy mascara, I have found grace for the many chapters of my life.

REFLECTION

Sharing your story doesn't earn immunity from difficult situations. We are commanded in 1 Corinthians 10:31 to *"do all to the glory of God."* All! Not just celebratory moments or those times when peace and happiness reign, but also when we're amidst the mundane, the slop, and even the days of grief. Throughout it all, we must *"do all to the glory of God."*

Have I arrived at that place? No. My story continues to be a work in process. Wrapping up this project, my days will continue to be challenged. My son will still be severely autistic, profoundly learning delayed, plagued with anxiety, and diagnosed with OCD and bipolar disorder. Only last night, my family endured a devastating violent meltdown at Ben's hands.

I do not write these words looking through rose-coloured glasses. Rather, my heart speaks from a deep-seated place, that moment more than fifty years ago when I trusted Christ as my Lord and Saviour.

Yes, I am prone to wander, but God in his faithfulness has loved me through it all. One day I will see my Saviour, and until then I will trust. For all my chapters have been stories of grace.

Tell me the story of Jesus,
write on my heart every word;
tell me the story most precious,
sweetest that ever was heard.
Tell how the angels, in chorus

sang as they welcomed his birth,
"Glory to God in the highest!
Peace and good tidings to earth."

Tell me the story of Jesus,
write on my heart every word;
tell me the story most precious,
sweetest that ever was heard.

Fasting alone in the desert,
tell of the days that he passed,
how for our sins he was tempted,
yet was triumphant at last.
Tell of the years of his labor,
tell of the sorrow he bore;
he was despised and afflicted,
homeless, rejected, and poor.

Tell of the cross where they nailed him,
writhing in anguish and pain;
tell of the grave where they laid him;
tell how he liveth again.
Love in that story so tender,
clearer than ever I see:
stay, let me weep while you whisper,
Love paid the ransom for me.[23]

---

[23] Fanny Crosby, "Tell Me the Story of Jesus," 1880.

Looking unto Jesus the author and finisher
of our faith; who for the joy that was set
before him endured the cross, despising the
shame, and is set down at the right hand
of the throne of God.
(Hebrews 12:2)

Who comforteth us in all our tribulation,
that we may be able to comfort them
which are in any trouble, by the comfort
wherewith we ourselves are
comforted of God.
(2 Corinthians 1:4)

Howbeit Jesus suffered him not, but saith
unto him, Go home to thy friends, and tell
them how great things the Lord hath done
for thee, and hath had compassion on thee.
(Mark 5:19)

Continue in prayer, and watch in the same
with thanksgiving; withal praying also for
us, that God would open unto us a door of
utterance, to speak the mystery of Christ,
for which I am also in bonds: that I may
make it manifest, as I ought to speak. Walk

in wisdom toward them that are without,
redeeming the time. Let your speech be
always with grace, seasoned with salt, that
ye may know how ye ought to answer every
man. (Colossians 4:2–6)

ACKNOWLEDGEMENTS

Thank you, to my church family, for praying, encouraging, and holding me accountable during the writing of this devotional.

Thank you, Kathy Butryn for so kindly crafting the Foreword to this book. Your words, "Lynn, I think you have a book in you", placed me on the journey of a lifetime.

Loving thanks to my mother, for being my "sounding board". With every rewrite, you have cheered me on to the finish line.

To my little family, you are the best! You have taught me to never give up on my dream, trust God with the details, and when the going gets tough, "order pizza!".

Special thanks to the staff at Word Alive Press for guiding me through the world of publishing. Your patience and direction have been a gift to me.

And to the person who has just read this book, I am honoured that you allowed me to share a little bit of God's faithfulness in my life. It is my deepest desire that all your chapters (especially the difficult ones) will be stories of grace.

Jude 24:25

Now unto him that is able to keep you from falling, and to present you faultless before the presence of his glory with exceeding joy, to the only wise God our Saviour, be glory and majesty, dominion and power, both now and ever. Amen.